Birding Arizona

What to know
Where to go

By Charles J. Babbitt

R.W. Morse Company
Olympia, Washington

Dedication

For Eleanor, Marissa and Elliott

Published by R.W. Morse Company, Olympia, Washington

Library of Congress Control Number: 2018956247
EAN 9780999073605
$19.95 Softcover
First Edition 2019
Copyright 2019 R.W. Morse Company

Printed: Imago Group, China

Author: Charles J. Babbitt

Executive Editor: Christina Duchesne Morse

Covers and Interior Design: Christina Merwin

Maps: Paul Biniasz

Cover Painting: Eleanor Babbitt

Grace's Warbler Cover
Grace's Warbler is a pine tree loving species with wide distribution around the state. A large percentage of its breeding range is confined to Arizona. One of only three North American songbirds named after women, it was named in honor of the sister of famed nineteenth century naturalist and ornithologist Elliott Coues who first discovered it near Prescott in 1864.

TABLE OF CONTENTS

TABLE OF CONTENTS

Introduction

For birders, there is no better place to live or visit than Arizona. The Grand Canyon State has more native bird species than just about any other state: over 550 bird species have been recorded here.

I was fortunate to be raised in Arizona and to have spent the greater part of my life looking for birds in its many and diverse habitats. My passion for birds has taken me from the top of the San Francisco Peaks in northern Arizona to the rolling grasslands of the San Rafael Valley along the US– Mexico border.

This book has been written in the hope that my 40 years of birding experience in Arizona will help birders find, identify, and appreciate its many bird species. It is written primarily for beginning and intermediate Arizona birders, as well as for visiting out-of-state birders of all skill levels. Each of the book's six chapters offers suggestions and ideas to help you find and appreciate the state's birdlife.

Chapter 1 takes you birding through the seasons as you learn about the many facets of Arizona bird migration. Migration (the seasonal movement of birds) is a paradox—it is at the same time both completely predictable and totally unpredictable. Often thought of as a spring and fall phenomenon, migration actually goes on in one form or another for much of the year. That's why many of the birds you see in July are different from those you find in December. Understanding and timing these bird movements is especially important for birders who enjoy chasing after and searching for rare and unusual species. This section concludes with a calendar to keep you out birding year-round.

Ways to improve your bird identification skills are discussed in **Chapter 2**. The first section offers a number of practical hints and suggestions to help you find and identify birds. The other two sections explain why birders learn and memorize birdsongs and calls (and suggests techniques and places for doing so) and explore how the careful study of beak size, shape, and color can be an important clue in bird identification. At the end of this chapter is a selected list of resources for beginners.

Chapter 3 introduces you to several select groups of Arizona birds. There are many birds one could write about, and I admit my list is a bit quirky. These birds were chosen because of my personal experience with them in the field and, most of all, my fondness for them. I never tire of listening to the complex, musical songs of the wrens or watching the antics of woodpeckers. I grew up around Pinyon Jays and Clark's Nutcrackers, two iconic birds of northern Arizona forests, and I anxiously await the arrival each spring of a special group of beautiful birds I've dubbed the "Arizona Warblers."

Arizona has many outstanding birding locations, many of which have been written about extensively. In **Chapter 4**, we take a tour of some of my favorite Arizona birding destinations, a number of which are in under-birded areas of northern Arizona. Some of these locations are well known, others less so, but all are unique and exciting places to visit. You'll also find out about some bird-rich spots in the Phoenix metropolitan area.

Many birders are counters and listers, i.e., they keep formal records of the bird species they see and identify. **Chapter 5** discusses the ways birders can have fun counting birds and, in the process, become "citizen scientists" who make important contributions to our knowledge of avian ecology and species distribution.

Chapter 6 is titled "Birding and the Environment." It discusses the many ways we benefit from the activity of birds, the importance of preserving habitat, and the lessons to be learned from our attempts to reintroduce three extirpated Arizona species: the California Condor, Masked Bobwhite, and Thick-billed Parrot.

Let's get started on a yearlong adventure as we go birding through the seasons.

Chapter 1: Birding Through the Seasons

In "Spring and Fall Migration," an early April morning in Phoenix sets the stage for a discussion of Arizona's spring and fall bird migration. "Strange Summer Visitors From the Gulf" will acquaint us with some of the unusual birds that find their way to Arizona from the Gulf of California during the summer monsoon. "Fall Shorebirding" takes you shorebirding, starting in late June and continuing through peak shorebird passage in early September. Our exploration through the seasons continues in "Winter Birding in Northern Arizona" with a discussion of special wintering birds that hardy birders can find in northern Arizona. "Winter Birding on the Colorado River" discusses the many interesting gulls, loons, grebes, ducks, and other waterbirds that spend the winter in Arizona, especially on the large lakes and reservoirs along the Colorado River. At the end of this chapter is a special calendar you can use to find birding opportunities in Arizona year-round.

Spring and Fall Migration

The sun had just come up as I walked out into my front yard in Phoenix early one morning last April. A late spring cold front had passed through the night before, leaving the sky cloudy with a slight wind blowing from the southwest.

Standing there, I could hear a chorus of singing birds. Most were familiar residents. A Northern Mockingbird that had been singing all night was still singing from atop a power pole. In the distance, there was the "whit-whit" call of a Curve-billed Thrasher and the repetitious three-note whistle of a Verdin. Occasionally, a Costa's Hummingbird would fly to the bright red blossoms of a neighbor's ocotillo and then retreat to a nearby perch. From time to time, I could detect the high-pitched "zing" of its song.

Besides the familiar residents, there were a number of recent arrivals. In just about every direction, White-winged Doves were singing. From the palo verde trees—now loaded with bright yellow blossoms—there were the rapid, sweet notes of a recently arrived Lucy's Warbler. A Hooded Oriole gave an occasional one-noted "wheet" call as it explored the dead fronds of a tall palm (no doubt looking for a nest site).

Suddenly, there was an unfamiliar "chip" note from a large acacia tree near the street. Out popped a Townsend's Warbler that had been moving about in the thick foliage. These beautiful black, yellow, and white warblers are not often seen in the lowland desert areas of Arizona in springtime. Most migrate through the state's higher mountain ranges. Townsend's Warbler is a "passage migrant," a bird that does not nest locally but only passes through on the way to its breeding grounds. Its presence that morning was a sure sign that spring migration was in full force.

Most Townsend's Warblers winter in Mexico. I have seen them in winter in humid oak forests in the state of Chiapas and in pine trees on the steep flanks of the Volcán de Colima. Their summer breeding and nesting grounds stretch along the Pacific coast from Oregon to Alaska. Watching it that morning, I wondered where this bird had spent the winter, how far it had traveled, and how far it still had to go.

The seasonal movement of migrating birds has always fascinated me. It's one of the reasons I like to go out and look for birds in the spring and fall. Those are particularly good times to look for seldom-seen and unusual species, and you can almost always count on a few surprises.

I also like migration for another reason. The sometimes mysterious (yet very predictable) comings and goings of migrating birds give me a sense of continuity, a connection to the past. That's why, year in and year out, I eagerly look forward to the passage of White-fronted Geese in mid-September, Franklin's Gulls in mid-April, Willets (which always seem to arrive at small ponds the first week of May), and Northern Waterthrushes (which always seem to arrive at small ponds the last week of August). There is really nothing mysterious about it, although it may seem that way. The birds are retracing ancient pathways etched across the continent since the retreat of glaciers at the end of the most recent ice age.

Bird migration in one form or another actually goes on for much of the year. While we often associate it with the dramatic, large-scale movement of birds between breeding and wintering grounds in spring and fall, a number of other, less obvious and more subtle movements occur at other seasons and for different reasons.

Sometimes, birds are adjusting to weather or food availability by making altitudinal changes—moving back and forth in their ranges between higher and lower elevations. This often happens in Arizona in fall and winter with species like Western Bluebird, Mountain Chickadee, and Red-breasted Nuthatch. On occasion, species irrupt in unexpected movements completely out of their normal ranges, responding to cone crop failures. Pinyon Jay and Clark's Nutcracker, and especially finches (Red Crossbill, Pine Siskin, and Cassin's Finch), are prone to irruption. In late summer, Gulf of California breeding species like Brown Pelican and Reddish Egret wander or scatter out of their normal ranges in post-breeding dispersal movements. One of the more unusual movements is that made by Phainopepla. These beautiful birds breed and nest in the Sonoran Desert at lower elevations in springtime, between February and April. As summer progresses and the supply of their favorite food, mistletoe berries, dwindles, many abandon desert areas and migrate into higher-elevation juniper, oak, and sycamore habitat, where they breed a second time.

The fact that bird migration is nearly always happening in some form makes it possible to look for different species throughout the year. However, spring is my favorite time to look for birds, for several reasons. In spring, birds are in their brightest and most colorful breeding ("alternate") plumage and are usually easier to identify. Also, birds sing in the springtime, making them easier to locate. Even rare migrant and vagrant species will often sing at least briefly as they pass through on their way to breeding grounds.

My birding year often begins in earnest in April, in agricultural fields west of Phoenix near Buckeye, Arizona. Cotton and alfalfa fields—particularly those that have been flooded with irrigation water—are often the resting place for migrating Swainson's Hawks. Dozens of these hawks can sometimes be spotted resting on raised berms in cotton and alfalfa fields. Swainson's Hawks migrate north every spring from their wintering grounds in northern Argentina. Some end their journey and nest in Arizona, but the majority fly on, nesting across a large swath of the western United States. As the cool air of an early April morning begins to heat up, you can often observe them in large flocks or "kettles" sometimes numbering in the hundreds, slowly circling on the rising thermals that will carry them north. They often fly so high you can barely make them out with the unaided eye. In one kettle, you can sometimes see all three color morphs: light, intermediate, and dark-phase birds.

Another favorite springtime trip is to look for migrating Townsend's and Hermit warblers in the mountain ranges of central Arizona: places like Mount Ord, the Pinal Mountains, and Mingus Mountain. These two warbler species are often found in small flocks, foraging high in the trees near the summits. In migration, Hermit and Townsend's warblers skip from the top of one mountain range to another as they migrate north from their wintering grounds in southern Mexico. Some springs, when weather disturbances are particularly strong, these beautiful warblers can be found away from the mountains, moving through the lowlands and along desert riparian corridors.

In the West, spring bird migration tends to be more dispersed and less concentrated than in the eastern United States. Western migrants often move north along riparian corridors. Think of spring migration as a river of birds flowing north. Some years, the river flows directly over Arizona, and it seems there are more birds and a greater variety of species. Other years, we only catch one side of the river, and migration is less impressive. It seems you can never be sure what spring migration will bring, but you can almost always count on a few surprises.

Birding Arizona

An example of the kind of surprises that can await birders during spring migration occurred in 1998. That year, there were an unusual number of Swainson's Thrushes, a highly migratory bird that moves north to its breeding grounds from southern Mexico and Central and South America. They showed up in large and unprecedented numbers, especially in the southeastern part of Arizona. A short hike up Sheelite Canyon in the Huachuca Mountains one cool May morning produced no fewer than four Swainson's Thrushes. Most years, you are lucky to find one.

The number of birds that migrate through North America each spring must be astounding. There are guesstimates of the numbers, but whatever it is, the total must be huge, when one considers these birds will fill up the forests of the contiguous United States, Canada, and Alaska. In Arizona alone, Tree Swallows numbering in the hundreds of thousands have been observed at Lake Havasu, migrating up the lower Colorado River Valley in springtime.

Much of the yearly bird migration takes place at night, and we are often unaware of its existence and extent unless, perhaps, you happen to be sleeping out-of-doors and hear calling flocks of birds as they pass overhead in the darkness.

Bird fallouts can give us an appreciation for the size of these natural movements. Along the Gulf coast of Texas and Louisiana, places like High Island can sometimes experience huge fallouts of trans-Gulf migrants in the spring. At these times, migrating birds hit the coastline and fall exhausted onto the shore, seemingly dripping from every bush and tree. In Arizona, we also have bird fallouts during migration from time to time.

Chapter 1

While ours are not as spectacular as those along the Gulf Coast, birders fortunate enough to experience one get an appreciation for the strength of spring and fall migration, as well as a chance to find some great birds. In the 1991 book *Birds of the Lower Colorado River Valley,* there is an account of an early May bird fallout due to bad weather conditions along the Colorado River in western Arizona. On May 9 and 10, 1977, the authors of that book counted over 650 migrants of 26 different species. Among them were a number of rare migrants and vagrants, including Black Swift, Prothonotary Warbler, Worm-eating Warbler, and Ovenbird.

A friend and I witnessed a similar but less impressive fallout one spring morning while birding in northeastern Arizona at Pasture Canyon near Tuba City. Strong storms the previous night forced down large numbers of migrating birds. What a sight it was! Scores of birds were hopping through tree branches, sitting on barbed-wire fences, and moving through the sagebrush. Among them were flycatchers, vireos, warblers, orioles, thrushes, and tanagers, all in fresh spring plumage.

Fall migration lasts longer and seems less hurried than spring migration. Birds tend to linger awhile, unlike during the more hectic and driven passage of springtime. There are also more birds in autumn, their numbers greatly increased by juveniles flying south for the first time.

One of my favorite places to watch fall migration is around the eastern Arizona communities of Springville and Eagar, in the White Mountains. These two towns sit in a bowl-shaped valley appropriately named Round Valley. On the horizon, Escudilla Mountain—immortalized in Aldo Leopold's classic *A Sand County*

Birding Arizona

Almanac and Sketches Here and There—rises to an elevation of nearly 11,000 feet. The Little Colorado River meanders through the valley, irrigating lush pastureland before turning north to its eventual confluence with the Colorado River.

In mid-September, this area teems with birds, many of them migrants. At times, small waves of Western Tanagers, Black-headed Grosbeaks, Lazuli Buntings, and Brewer's Sparrows push through on their way south. It seems like birds are everywhere. Trips to the area can sometimes produce as many as 11 warbler species, 10 sparrow species, and up to five species of *Empidonax* flycatchers, or "empids": Willow, Gray, Cordilleran, Hammond's, and Dusky. Some of these fall birds present significant identification challenges. Besides juvenile birds in unfamiliar plumage, many adult species—especially warblers—are in drab winter or basic plumage. Field guides often refer to them generically as "confusing fall warblers."

My favorite spot to look for fall migrants and occasional vagrants in this area is South Fork, about five miles outside Eagar. South Fork is a cold, clear tributary of the Little Colorado River that alternates fast-flowing riffles with quiet, beaver-dammed ponds. The streamside is a dense tangle of willow, dogwood, and locust. In mid-September, plants like elderberry and wolfberry are loaded with berries that migrating birds eat. The area has an interesting mix of habitat and a variety of trees, including ponderosa pine, cottonwood, pinyon pine, and juniper. No doubt this plant diversity is what helps attract some of the rare and unusual migrant and vagrant birds that have been found here, including Orchard Oriole, Rose-breasted Grosbeak, Northern Parula, Chestnut-sided Warbler, American Redstart, Eastern Phoebe, Scarlet Tanager, and one autumn, a White-eared Hummingbird that had strayed far from its usual southeastern Arizona range. Nearby Becker Lake is one of the most reliable places in Arizona to see a Dickcissel. These rare migrants pass through the area with clocklike regularity each fall around September 15. Their long journey will take them to wintering grounds in Venezuela.

The comings and goings of migrating birds, especially in spring and fall, can be so predictable you can almost set your calendar by their arrival and departure. This is especially true with neotropical migrants that return to our area to nest in springtime after wintering in Mexico and Central and South America. Every spring, White-winged Doves return in the first week of April, singing their loud "who cooks for you" song. Their arrival coincides with the blooming of ocotillo, whose seeds are one of the doves' favorite foods. After spending the summer, White-winged Doves almost magically disappear right around September 1. It seems one day they are here, and the next day they're gone. Actually, the yearly return and departure of birds, including many neotropical nesting species, has nothing to do with magic; it's a result of the birds' response to a number of environmental clues, including changes in temperature and daylight.

Likewise, there are cases of an individual bird returning to the same area on almost the same date year after year. It is often a neotropical migrant returning from the south for the breeding season, as was the case with a Flame-colored Tanager in Madera Canyon. That bird returned regularly for about eight consecutive years, usually arriving punctually the last week of March. Another tanager, a possible Western × Summer hybrid, returned to the Verde Valley for around five consecutive years, being spotted each spring about the third week of May.

Birding Arizona

The same thing can happen with passage migrants. One late May afternoon, I observed an Eastern Kingbird, a rare migrant, perched on a dead snag at Becker Lake. The next year on exactly the same date, there was an Eastern Kingbird on the same snag—more than likely the same bird, stopping on its way north to breed.

If you want to set your calendar by the arrival of birds, watch large sycamores and cottonwoods along creeks and streams in central Arizona. Every spring, right around March 15, Common Black-Hawks return to these riparian areas after spending the winter in Mexico. Shortly after their return, you hear their loud, whistled warning calls whenever you near a nest site.

Rufous Hummingbirds, non-nesting but regular visitors to Arizona, can almost always be counted on to appear in fall migration the second week of July, often stopping briefly at flowers or feeders. These birds are the first trickle of what will become a river of migrating hummingbirds that reaches its peak in early September. They make a long fall journey that takes them from breeding grounds in British Columbia and southeastern Alaska over some of the most mountainous and arid lands in the world to wintering grounds in southern Mexico.

The seasonal regularity and predictability of migrating birds helps birders who want to go out and look for rare and unusual species. Cumulative sight records will often reveal recurring patterns of migration or vagrancy. These patterns often involve small numbers of birds and very brief windows of time. Some occur annually with fairly consistent regularity. Anticipating them, birders can go out and look for that rare species they've always wanted to see.

For example, Arizona is occasionally host to Heermann's

Gull, a gull that breeds in the Gulf of California and moves north to spend the winter along the Pacific coast. Most state records are of single birds, and most sightings are very brief. In fact, Heermann's Gulls are known as "one-day wonders." Sight records show that these gulls migrate through Arizona in the spring in very small numbers, often in early April. Sight records also show another discernible spurt of sightings in November, as they move north in the fall.

Sabine's Gull is a small gull that breeds in the high Arctic. Most migrate in autumn well off the Pacific and Atlantic coasts. Almost every year, however, some of these gulls also make their way to Arizona and are found on large and small bodies of water. Most are juveniles, which usually appear right around the middle of September.

At Yaki and Lipan points on the South Rim of the Grand Canyon, hawk watchers count migrating raptors passing over the canyon each fall. Among them are always a very small number of Broad-winged Hawks, a small woodland buteo. During a brief window of time beginning in mid-September, a few Broad-winged Hawks pass by, with the peak time to see them around September 29.

Native Americans and our farming and ranching forefathers were no doubt attuned to and keenly aware of the seasonal arrival and departure of migrating birds. Among the Pima Indians, for example, the arrival of the Northern Harrier or "Vakav" is a sign that winter is coming. Today, we have celebrations honoring these natural events. The best-known, of course, is the return of swallows to the old mission of San Juan Capistrano in California.

Birding Arizona

Cliff Swallows that pass the winter months in Argentina return to the mission around the middle of March to begin building their mud nests. At Boyce Thompson Arboretum near Superior, Arizona, there are annual "Buzzard Days" celebrating the spring return and fall departure of migrating Turkey Vultures.

In the following sections, other facets of Arizona bird migration will be discussed as we continue birding through the seasons. Among them are the midsummer dispersal of Gulf of California birds into Arizona, fall shorebird migration, the winter influx of northerly breeding species into northern Arizona, and the annual influx of wintering waterbirds along the Colorado River. Readers are encouraged, if they so desire, to go immediately to the section of this chapter that corresponds to the current time of year.

Strange Summer Visitors From the Gulf

A Magnificent Frigatebird, its long, angular wings outstretched, suddenly appeared out of nowhere, floating slowly through the cloud-filled sky toward water shimmering in the distance. No, I was not watching it from a sandy beach along the Gulf of California that hot July morning. In fact, I was standing about a mile from the shoreline of a large, temporary lake—the result of heavy winter runoff—behind Painted Rock Dam near Gila Bend, Arizona.

The Magnificent Frigatebird is a sea pirate, known for its aerial agility and habit of robbing food from gulls and other seabirds. It seemed oddly out of place flying over the desert that morning, but Arizona birders have come to expect strange and unexpected visitors from the Gulf of California starting around mid-July each year.

Every summer as the humidity rises and the Arizona monsoon begins to bubble, the state is visited by wandering, post-breeding adult and juvenile birds that disperse north and east from the Gulf of California. These birds find their way to large and small bodies of water around Arizona, arriving either directly from the Gulf of California or from concentrations of birds that first dispersed from the gulf to the nearby Salton Sea. Both the Gulf of California and Salton Sea (a large inland body of water in southern California) are just a few hundred miles away from Arizona, which is a fairly short hop for a strong flier like a Magnificent Frigatebird.

Brown Pelicans are famous for their post-breeding dispersal from the Gulf of California. These large seabirds find their way to Arizona just about every summer, although the numbers vary considerably from year to year, from just a few dozen to several hundred. Virtually all of them are inexperienced juvenile birds. They can show up anywhere where there is water and sometimes where there isn't any water, landing in the middle of the desert on roadways or even in backyards. Several years ago, one was found at a bus stop in Phoenix. These young, inexperienced birds are often in a weakened and exhausted condition, in need of care if they are to survive. In the summer of 2011, Liberty Wildlife rescued eight juvenile brown pelicans and transferred them to SeaWorld San Diego for rehabilitation and release.

Depending on the food supply, some Brown Pelicans linger in Arizona into autumn, and occasionally a few can be found in winter on large lakes such as Lake Havasu and even Tempe Town

Lake. The arrival of juvenile Brown Pelicans is often associated with weather disturbances and strong prevailing winds from the Gulf of California.

Even more remarkable are very rare late-summer visits by two pelican relatives, Brown and Blue-footed boobies. These gregarious seabirds are often observed fishing in the Gulf of California, where they make spectacular headlong dives into the ocean, their long wings folding back a split second before the bird hits the water. In 1990 and 1996, both species showed up at small artificial lakes in the Phoenix area, although in Arizona they are most frequently seen on large lakes or other bodies of water along the Colorado River.

Herons and other large wading birds are known for wandering away from their breeding grounds and habitats after they finish nesting, which is known as "post-breeding dispersal." Starting in midsummer, there usually are scattered sightings of rare and uncommon heron species around the state. These include species that breed in the Gulf of California, such as Little Blue Heron, Tricolored Heron, and Reddish Egret.

These birds can disperse widely and show up in very unlikely places. I remember seeing my first state Little Blue Heron at Ganado Lake on Navajo tribal lands in the far northeastern part of Arizona. (Many birders keep a list of birds they have seen in a particular state. This was the first time I'd seen a Little Blue Heron in Arizona.) These rarer heron species are sometimes found in flocks with more common resident species, such as Great Blue Heron, Great Egret, and Snowy Egret. All heron species are marvelously adapted to stalking and hunting fish and amphibian prey, which they spear or seize with their daggerlike bills.

One of my favorite wading birds is not a heron but a Wood Stork, a rare summer visitor from the Gulf of California or Salton Sea. They are sometimes found standing quietly in the shallows of a lake or pond. Wood Storks have long, decurved bills, which they open and place in the water. When a fish or amphibian swims between the bill tips, the bill instantly snaps shut, seizing the prey. Adult birds have bald, blackish heads that give them a prehistoric look, perhaps betraying their dinosaur lineage more than is true of other bird species. Seeing one of these big birds flying with outstretched head and feet, I am reminded of some ancient flying reptile from the Jurassic period.

One of the most unusual and beautiful wading birds found in Arizona every few years is the Roseate Spoonbill. These rare summer visitors are often juvenile birds that are mostly white or slightly pinkish in color. They lack the bright, roseate hues of adult birds, and their head is feathered instead of bald. Spoonbills have a large spatulate or spoon-shaped bill, from which the species gets its name. They mostly feed in shallow water, sweeping their bill from side to side, stirring up water to flush and capture prey.

Another late-summer visitor with an even more bizarre-looking bill and hunting strategy is the Black Skimmer. This member of the tern family is the only North American bird that has a lower mandible that is longer than the upper mandible. Skimmers fly over the water with the lower part of their narrow, blade-like bill slicing through the water. When the lower mandible comes into contact with a fish, the upper snaps shut. There have been fewer than a dozen records of this bird in Arizona, some of which are believed to come from a small breeding population at the Salton Sea.

Another tern species, the Elegant Tern, sometimes finds its way to Arizona from the Gulf of California during summertime. More than 90 percent of the entire Elegant Tern population breeds on Isla Rasa, a tiny island in the gulf that is more or less on the same latitude as Hermosillo, Sonora. I was fortunate to see the first state record of this species at Painted Rock Dam near Gila Bend in 1988. In June 2009, there was a remarkable mini-invasion of these shaggy-crested terns into Arizona, with at least five individuals being seen at three different locations in the southeastern part of the state. This invasion followed the abandonment of the nesting colony on Isla Rasa due to rising sea-surface temperatures and resultant lack of prey. Arrival of the terns coincided with strong southwest winds from the gulf.

Once in a great while, the Gulf of California can almost literally dump its birds into Arizona lakes. This has happened on a few rare occasions with the late-summer passage of tropical weather systems moving northward from the gulf. These events can turn birders into storm chasers.

In 1997, tropical storm Nora came up the gulf and crossed into Arizona with tropical-force winds, which rapidly dissipated as the storm moved north along the Colorado River. In the process, seabirds swept up from the gulf by the storm's powerful winds were dumped into Lake Havasu.

The fallout of birds from this event was a bonanza for the state's birders. Many were able to see first state records or birds recorded in the state only once or twice before. Among the most notable were hundreds of Least Storm-Petrels and scores of slightly larger Black Storm-Petrels. These highly pelagic (ocean-going) birds are rarely, if ever, found away from their saltwater environment.

Storm-Petrels and Shearwaters belong to a group of seabirds called "tubenoses," so named for the large tubular nasal passages on top of their bills, which (it is believed) help them smell and locate patchily distributed food out on the ocean. After Nora's passage, there were reports of other, even rarer tubenose species on Lake Havasu, including Leach's Storm-Petrel and a Black-vented Shearwater.

The most recent of these rare events occurred in September 2016. Hurricane Newton formed off the Mexican coast on September 5, 2016, and moved up the Baja Peninsula as a Category 1 hurricane. After crossing the Gulf of California, it moved north-northwest, crossing into Arizona as a weakening post-tropical cyclone that brought a narrow swath of rain and wind, mostly into Pima and Cochise counties. Like Nora 17 years earlier, Newton brought with it a number of seabirds never seen before in Arizona, including a Wedge-tailed Shearwater, several Wedge-rumped Storm-Petrels, and rarest of all, a Juan Fernandez Petrel.

The annual summer dispersal of birds from the Gulf of California is a natural phenomenon that is not fully understood. Besides the tendency for both young and adult birds to move away from breeding grounds and habitats after the breeding season, other factors often are cited as reasons for these movements. They include food shortages caused by sea temperature changes, overproduction of young birds, and the propensity of juvenile birds to wander.

Birding Arizona

What is clear, however, is that weather is frequently a factor that brings dispersing birds from the gulf. Beginning in late June or early July, a shift in the direction of prevailing winds, from west to south or southwest, causes a change in Arizona's weather pattern. This shift brings moist gulf air into the state, causing the buildup of thunderstorms as summer progresses. These southerly winds from the gulf and the storms they create greatly facilitate the inland movement of birds, particularly juveniles that have recently fledged and are no longer being fed by their parents.

Arizona birders and naturalists have a unique opportunity each year to find and observe rare and unusual species that disperse from the Gulf of California and Salton Sea. Next summer as the humidity rises and the cumulus clouds of the monsoon begin to build, keep an eye on the horizon. You just might see a long-winged sea pirate riding southerly winds across the desert.

Footnote: The reservoir behind Painted Rock Dam has been dry for many years, a reminder of just how severe a drought the Southwest has experienced the last two decades. During the wet decades of the 1970s, 1980s, and part of the 1990s, runoff down the Gila River would sometimes turn the reservoir into the second-largest water body in the state. The borrow pit lake in front of the dam has also been dry in recent years. When there is water, however, the lakes in front and behind the dam can provide outstanding birding.

Chapter 1

Fall Shorebirding

Two shorebirders, spotting scopes in hand, struggle through a dense thicket of tamarisk trees toward water rapidly evaporating under the midday sun. They're looking for shorebirds flying south from breeding grounds in the high Arctic of Canada and Alaska. Their hope is that some have stopped to linger at a small pond along Interstate 8 outside Gila Bend, Arizona. It is mid-August, and across North America, fall shorebird migration is underway.

Shimmering heat waves make spotting scope–viewing difficult, but eventually, birds come into focus. About two-dozen shorebirds are feeding along the water's edge, picking and probing in the dark mud with their long, tubular bills. Among them are juvenile Western Sandpipers sporting bright rufous scapulars, a scaly-backed juvenile Baird's Sandpiper, Least Sandpipers, Long-billed Dowitchers, and a lone Semipalmated Plover that occasionally stops to look around alertly as it forages across the mud. Out in deeper water, two Wilson's Phalaropes spin in circles, picking at the water with long, pointed bills.

Spotting scopes soon focus on a bird at the corner of the pond. It is noticeably different—a large, long-winged, rather dumpy-looking shorebird with rusty red feathers throughout its breast. It is a Red Knot, a rare vagrant whose 9,000-mile fall migration takes it from Arctic breeding grounds to wintering grounds at the tip of South America. For these diehard shorebirders, the Red Knot is the bird of the day; perhaps the bird of the season.

The desert Southwest isn't a place that normally comes to mind when you think about shorebirding. Sparsely vegetated desert landscapes broiling under a relentless sun are a far cry from the cool tidal flats, sandy beaches, and watery marshes one associates with these birds. Shorebirds often pass through unnoticed, flying high over the deserts or stopping only briefly to rest. Driving along Interstate 8 toward California in the heat of summer, one would hardly suspect a major migration is underway: that is, until you look for water.

Water is hard to find in the desert Southwest, particularly in central and western Arizona, where much of it gets used up by municipal and agricultural water users and the area's innumerable golf courses. Aside from a handful of well-known and generally reliable spots, suitable shorebird habitat is always scarce. Desert shorebirders know, however, that even a little water in this arid environment is often enough to attract an impressive variety of shorebirds that will stop to rest and feed if water levels are right.

A variety of places can attract migrating shorebirds, including flooded alfalfa fields, recharge ponds, irrigation canals and impoundments, ephemeral ponds charged by late-summer rains, and sludge and containment ponds at water treatment plants and dairy cattle–feeding operations. Shorebirders have to be resourceful. Many of these far-flung water sources are only temporary, and new places often have to be found each year. A good shorebirding spot one week can be completely dried up two weeks later. One fall, a broken water main west of Phoenix sent a flood of water into a nearby gravel pit, creating excellent shorebird habitat for the next three weeks.

Shorebirds migrate through southwestern deserts at the very hottest and driest time of year. This means that shorebirders not only have to be resourceful, they have to be tough. Daytime temperatures in these areas can sometimes reach 115 degrees. Besides the heat, shorebirders often have to contend with swarms of flies, near-suffocating smells from wastewater treatment and containment ponds, and heat waves rising off the water that can make using a spotting scope nearly impossible. At times, sun-heated spotting scopes and tripods can become almost too hot to carry.

On occasion, shorebirding can be downright hazardous. Shorebirders sometimes have to cross drying mud flats, especially on ephemeral ponds and lakes like Painted Rock Reservoir near Gila Bend. Shorebirders walking across mudflats to scope for birds can suddenly find themselves knee-deep in mud as sun-baked cracks in the ground give way under their feet.

Fall shorebird migration actually begins in early summer, often by the end of June or in early July. The last Arctic-bound shorebirds headed north have barely passed through when the first southbound adults begin to appear. A few years ago, an adult Baird's Sandpiper found at the Glendale recharge pond in mid-June left a friend and me wondering if it was a rare spring migrant going north or an early adult returning south.

By early July, however, returning adult shorebirds begin to appear in steadily growing numbers. Many of these Arctic breeders are in worn breeding plumage. They are sometimes joined by more numerous migrating Great Basin breeders like Wilson's Phalarope, Long-billed Curlew, and Willet, along with other waterbirds such as White-faced Ibis and Caspian, Forster's and Black terns. Female Wilson's Phalaropes sometimes begin arriving as early as late June, leaving the males to tend the juveniles back on the breeding grounds.

One of my favorite Arctic breeders, the Stilt Sandpiper, sometimes shows up in mid-July. I remember watching one of these elegant waders standing in belly-deep water near the alkali-crusted edge of an evaporating irrigation ditch. It still retained most of its breeding plumage - deep chestnut-red on its face and head and striking black barring on the chest and belly. Another Arctic breeder, the Greater Yellowlegs, can show up even earlier, sometimes in early July. They also retain much of their breeding plumage, especially the dark barring on the flanks. When you see these birds in the scorching heat at the edge of a sludge pond, it's difficult to imagine that a few weeks earlier, they may have been on Arctic tundra or in a northern muskeg bog surrounded by black spruce trees.

The pace of shorebird migration quickens at the end of July. This is the time when juveniles begin to appear. Adult shorebirds leave their Arctic breeding grounds first, followed by the juveniles a few weeks later. These young birds are undertaking their first daunting journey southward. Among the initial arrivals are juvenile Least Sandpipers and juvenile Western Sandpipers with their distinctive bright rufous scapulars. Juvenile shorebirds often have a crisp, scaly-looking back with a buffy breast. This is the case with both juvenile Baird's Sandpipers and juvenile Pectoral Sandpipers. Both Baird's and Pectorals are rare in Arizona in the springtime, with most adults migrating north through the middle and eastern parts of the continent. Beginning in July, however, numbers of juvenile Baird's Sandpipers begin migrating through the Southwest, followed by juvenile Pectoral Sandpipers about a month later.

The end of July is also when two uncommon shorebirds, juvenile Short-billed Dowitchers and Semipalmated Sandpipers, are sometimes found by sharp-eyed shorebirders. Both species can easily be overlooked among the more common and expected Long-billed Dowitchers and Western Sandpipers.

Desert shorebirders often face the same challenge with shorebirds as with gulls—a lack of familiarity. Birders along the coasts are accustomed to seeing scores of migrating shorebirds in a variety of molts and plumages, making it easy to compare their relative sizes, shapes, and ages. In the desert Southwest, however, many fewer shorebirds are present at any given time. Shorebirds are often found in small numbers or as single birds in unlikely places under difficult weather and lighting conditions. Lack of experience and unfamiliarity make it easier for a rare species to slip by unnoticed or for a more common species to be misidentified.

Some of the tougher and more unpleasant places to shorebird are containment ponds at dairy cattle–feeding operations. These "slop ponds," as they're called by local birders, can produce interesting shorebirds on occasion, including such species as Black-bellied Plover, Snowy Plover, Willet, Dunlin, and, several years ago, a Red Phalarope, that most pelagic of the phalarope species. In late September 2013, a Sharp-tailed Sandpiper was found at a dairy slop pond in western Maricopa County, and in July 2016, a Hudsonian Godwit made an appearance just up the road at another pond.

Black-necked Stilt, American Avocet, and Killdeer are three locally breeding shorebird species often encountered by shorebirders along the banks and edges of these ponds. All three species lay their eggs in shallow, scooped-out depressions on open ground, often during the hottest part of summer.

I'm always amazed at how they manage to raise their young under such extreme conditions. Actually, they do quite well. These birds sit on their exposed but well-camouflaged eggs, not to keep them warm, but to keep them cool. The stilts and avocets go even further, soaking their breast feathers in water to aid in the egg-cooling process. Shorebirders who get too close to these nests are often confronted by loud scolding calls, occasional swooping attacks, and in the case of the Killdeer, the classic "broken wing" feint.

Some relief from the Southwest's oppressive heat comes in early August with the onset of Arizona's monsoon. A shift in the prevailing winds from west to south or southwest brings moist air from the Gulf of California. These prevailing winds and the storms they create not only produce rain, but they can bring a variety of dispersing birds from the gulf and nearby Salton Sea, including species like Wood Stork, Black Skimmer, Little Blue Heron, Reddish Egret, and on rare occasions, Roseate Spoonbill. Juvenile Brown Pelicans disperse from the gulf every year at this time, sometimes in large numbers. Shorebirders are sometimes amazed to see a Brown Pelican quietly floating in a small pond or flying along a highway. It's enough to make a birder think he's been standing in the sun too long.

Two of the more reliable places to look for shorebirds in this arid environment are irrigated alfalfa fields and sod farms. There are very few of the latter in Arizona, but they can produce special shorebird sightings. The state's first Pacific Golden-Plover and an early July Upland Sandpiper were both found on a sod farm near

Chapter 1

Picacho.

When you visit alfalfa fields, the trick is to drive around and find places where irrigation water is being turned out into fields at the level of a few inches deep. Long-billed Curlew, Greater and Lesser yellowlegs, Long-billed Dowitcher, and Pectoral Sandpiper are often attracted to these areas. Sometimes, you can let the birds find the right habitat for you. More than once, I've found good shorebirding spots by following passing flocks of Long-billed Curlew or White-faced Ibis and watching to see where they land. Some very rare shorebirds that have been found in alfalfa fields include Ruff, Upland Sandpiper, and Arizona's first Buff-breasted Sandpiper. Solitary Sandpipers can sometimes be spotted in the bottoms of drying irrigation canals in these areas.

The annual fall shorebird migration reaches its height at the end of August. During this peak time, you can watch an almost continual turnover of migrating shorebirds at a few well-known locations like the Glendale recharge ponds and Gilbert Water Ranch near Phoenix, and Lake Cochise near Willcox in southeastern Arizona. On a good day, shorebirders can sometimes find over 20 different species. The list of fall shorebirds recorded in Arizona is impressive and continues to grow. Some of the rare and uncommon Arctic migrants found in Arizona in the fall include Ruddy Turnstone, Red Knot, Wandering Tattler, Sanderling, Red Phalarope, Ruff, and American and Pacific Golden-plovers.

At times, desert shorebirding can be difficult, but in spite of occasional hardships, it's also fun and always unpredictable. You never know from year to year what is going to show up and where. The Curlew Sandpiper is a species that many think is overdue in

Arizona. This highly migratory Siberian breeder could well show up some fall, perhaps in the central or western part of the state, stopping briefly at some water treatment plant or containment pond. More than likely, it will be a buffy-breasted, scaly-backed juvenile on its first solo journey southward. We'll be watching for it.

Winter Birding in Northern Arizona

High, thin notes announced their arrival. A small, compact flock of birds landed in an apple tree and began feeding on dried apples left over from the previous fall. It was a rare sight and one I will never forget. The birds clinging to the branches swaying in the cold February wind were Bohemian Waxwings. Elegant nomads with sleek crests, Bohemian Waxwings breed in northern Canada and Alaska. Although they're known to wander great distances in winter in search of food, their irregular and unpredictable movements rarely bring them as far south as Arizona. In 1984, however, they found their way to the Flagstaff area. By mid-March, their numbers had grown to where they were flying all over town, visiting fruit trees and perching in blue spruce and other ornamental trees in city parks. Just as suddenly, toward the end of March, they disappeared. Since that memorable winter more than 30 years ago, they have not returned.

Winter is an exciting time to be out birding in northern Arizona. Hardy birders willing to brave frigid temperatures and snow are sometimes rewarded with species rarely seen elsewhere in the state or at other times of year. Beginning in November, there is usually an influx of rare or uncommon northern-breeding species into northern Arizona. A few are typically found each winter. They include species like Northern Shrike, Black-capped Chickadee, Lapland Longspur, Rough-legged Hawk, Harris's Sparrow, American Tree Sparrow, and Black Rosy-Finch. In recent years, northern Arizona has had midwinter first state records for two such species: White-winged Crossbill and Common Redpoll.

Cassin's Finch is a species that can sometimes be found in northern Arizona in good numbers in winter. These finches, at first glance, look similar to the House Finch. What immediately separates them, however, is the male's distinctive square cap, which is a bright red color. In fact, that square red cap can sometimes cause novice birders to mistake them for the Common Redpoll. Small numbers of Cassin's Finches breed in northern Arizona, most notably on the Kaibab Plateau. In winter, particularly in years when there is an influx of Cassin's Finches from regions north of the state, they can be quite common. Other years, they are almost entirely absent. In those years when they are around, Cassin's Finches should be looked for in subdivisions and riparian areas, and at feeders.

Evening Grosbeak is another finch species birders should look for in northern Arizona in winter. These large finches have a massive, pale bill. Like Cassin's Finches, they tend to be irregular and unpredictable, but in flight years, they can be fairly easy to find. These striking yellow, black, and white birds should be sought in residential areas, where flocks can sometimes be spotted perched in bare, deciduous trees or even at feeders. Flocks of feeding Evening Grosbeaks can often be found by listening for their calls: busy, high-pitched notes reminiscent of those of House Sparrows.

Wintertime also sees an influx of Dark-eyed Juncos. Some

flocks can have up to four different races of junco: Oregon, Pink-sided, Gray-headed, and Slate-colored. These can be both challenging and fun to identify. They're an example of speciation, the process by which—through mutation, hybridization, and geographic isolation—new species arise from existing species. Over time, these forms have diverged from their ancestral stock, evolving distinct plumage and often occupying different summer breeding ranges. Eventually, one or all four of these races may become full-fledged species.

In addition to bringing an influx of northerly breeding birds, winter is also the time birders can find more common resident species in impressive numbers, feeding on plants like juniper and Russian olive. In winter, birds often move from higher elevations to lower elevations in search of food, and their numbers become concentrated. One reliable place to search for these elevational migrants is in dense thickets of Russian olive. This introduced exotic plant has spread throughout northern Arizona. Typically planted as a windbreak, it has invaded many areas, where it has outcompeted much of the native vegetation.

In spite of its bad reputation, Russian olive attracts and sustains birds during the harsh winter months. In fact, Russian olive thickets can be one of the most productive places in northern Arizona to bird in the winter. Species like American Goldfinch, Pine Siskin, Mountain Chickadee, and Townsend's Solitaire are often found in these thickets. On occasion, birders are treated to large flocks of Cedar Waxwing and Mountain and Western bluebirds feeding on the plant's small, grainy fruits.

American Robin is another species that can sometimes

be found in impressive flocks in wintertime. During the winter of 1994–1995, there was an exceptional mast crop of juniper berries in the pinyon-juniper woodlands of northern Arizona. There were so many berries that the trees looked like they were covered with snow. It did not take long for birds, particularly American Robins, to find them. Observers counted thousands of robins feeding in the trees. Near Wupatki National Monument, there were reports of wave upon wave of robins flying overhead in search of berries and water. At times, as many as 50 birds would fly up from individual juniper trees. There were similar reports of large numbers of congregating American Robins near Flagstaff in 2008.

The lakes south of Flagstaff can provide excellent birding in wintertime, especially in late winter as ducks and other waterfowl begin migrating north. Every year for about 20 years, I've led an annual Maricopa Audubon Society field trip in mid-March to Upper and Lower Lake Mary and Mormon Lake. The star attractions of these trips are wintering Bald Eagles, which we almost always find perched in trees or snags along lake edges. These are not our desert-nesting Bald Eagles found along the Salt, Gila, and Verde river systems, but eagles that breed in the northern Rocky Mountains and arrive as winter visitors in autumn. Although primarily fish eaters, Bald Eagles also feed on carrion or just about anything else available. On one trip, we watched an adult Bald Eagle walk out onto the ice on Upper Lake Mary and grab an American Coot that was swimming in an ice-free pocket of water.

These late-winter trips are an especially good time to see waterfowl. By mid-March, the lakes are mostly ice-free, and migrating birds are moving through. Large numbers of Canada Geese often stop in at Upper Lake Mary and Mormon Lake on their long journey to northern breeding grounds. Some tours produced an occasional Snow Goose or an even rarer Greater White-fronted Goose. On one memorable trip, we spotted two adult Tundra Swans walking through snowdrifts that had piled up on the ice on Mormon Lake. At a distance, the two white swans blended in perfectly with the snow, with only their black beaks and feet giving them away.

It's not unusual to spot as many as 15 different duck species on the lakes. Some of the rarer and more unusual have included Red-breasted and Hooded mergansers, Greater Scaup, and Common Goldeneye. On a trip in 2013, we spotted a Eurasian Wigeon on Mormon Lake. This male sported a beautiful russet-red head and a yellowish forehead and crown. It was one of only a few records of this species for northern Arizona away from the Colorado River.

On these trips, we always stop along the highway at the Mormon Lake overlook. Over the years, a number of rare wintering species have been found here, including Short-eared Owl and Northern Shrike. In winter, the Northern Shrikes found in northern Arizona are as likely to be juveniles as they are adults. To me, the juveniles are more interesting and also easier to identify. Juvenile Northern Shrikes are brownish in color, with distinct barring or scaling on the chest. A rounded head and slight mask give them an almost clownish appearance.

The windswept overlook at Mormon Lake is a great place to check for wintering raptors. On several field trips, we spotted Northern Rough-legged Hawks. These Arctic visitors sometimes hover nearly motionless, their heads pointed into a wind that can blow with gale-like force across the lake. On a trip in 2012, we saw three different Rough-legged Hawks at this spot. On other occasions, we found different raptors, including Golden Eagles and Ferruginous and Red-tailed hawks.

Our groups always stop at Mormon Lake village and lodge. This area can be very productive in wintertime. In the large pines near the lodge, we look and listen for Red Crossbills and Cassin's Finches. On several trips, we viewed flocks of Evening Grosbeaks, which we almost always found by first hearing their calls. This is also a good place to look for that most beautiful of all the Arizona woodpeckers, Lewis's Woodpecker. We sometimes spot them on pine snags or in small groves of Gambel oak in the residential area.

These excursions are just late enough in winter to get a few early spring migrants. One year, we spotted a Long-billed Dowitcher and a Wilson's Snipe—a strange sight as they walked through the snow at the edge of a small pond near Mormon Lake. On another occasion, we had an early Violet-green Swallow, its metallic green plumage glinting in the sunlight as it turned and glided against a backdrop of snow.

Following our circuit around Mormon Lake, we usually travel the 16 miles north to Ashurst Lake to look for Pinyon Jays, which we almost always see (or at least hear in the distance). This is also a reliable place to look for Juniper Titmice.

Sometimes, we conclude these field trips with a nighttime drive up the Snowbowl Road north of Flagstaff to look for Northern Saw-whet Owls. These tiny owls, which breed on the San Francisco Peaks, begin calling in earnest in March and April. Following their incessant calls through knee-deep snow in the hopes of spotting one brings any winter birding trip to an exciting conclusion.

Winter Birding on the Colorado River

Arizona is host to an impressive influx of waterbirds that withdraw from colder northerly climes in autumn and winter. Many of these migrating birds visit the state only briefly, but some end up overwintering. Over the years, birders have found a variety of migrating and wintering waterbirds, including ducks, loons, grebes, and gulls.

Although they can occur just about anywhere, these birds are usually found on large bodies of water. The best locations to look for them are places like Lake Pleasant and Saguaro Lake, and especially on reservoirs and below dams along the Colorado River. These include lakes Powell, Mead, Mohave, and Havasu.

By far the most frequently visited and easiest of these lakes to bird is Havasu. Lake Havasu is a sprawling, 19,000-acre lake behind Parker Dam, which was constructed in the 1930s. The lake straddles the Arizona-California border, with roughly half the lake in one state and half in the other. It has an irregular shoreline with many coves and inlets. Much of this lake is inaccessible to birders unless they go out in a boat. There are, however, a number of locations on shore that are accessible to birders using spotting scopes.

From an environmental point of view, construction of Parker Dam and other dams along the Colorado River was a disaster. Their construction tamed the mighty Colorado River, but in the process impounded and drained away its water, destroying hundreds of miles of riparian habitat that extended all the way to the Gulf of California. What we're left with today are several large, mostly sterile reservoirs, connected to each other by deep-water channels and canals.

These dams and the large man-made lakes behind them have, however, created new habitats for bird species not regularly seen here before their construction, including a number associated with deep water and oceanic habitat. Many now winter on these large lakes, providing birders an opportunity to see species rarely found elsewhere in the state.

One example is Barrow's Goldeneye. When published in 1963, *The Birds of Arizona* listed Barrow's Goldeneye as a hypothetical species; that is, a species that has been reported with substantial documentation but not supported by a specimen, photograph, or multiple observations. Since 1973, however, these beautiful ducks have been found regularly below Parker, Davis, and Glen Canyon dams. The easiest place to see Barrow's Goldeneye is below Parker Dam. They can be seen there every winter, diving and feeding in the deep, cold water alongside the more numerous Common Goldeneye. In the evening, many goldeneye leave the fast-flowing river and fly up onto the calm waters of the Bill Williams Delta. Here, they often join flocks of Greater Scaup and Red-breasted Merganser, two more deepwater ducks that are hard to find in much of Arizona but can easily be seen either below Parker Dam or on Lake Havasu.

Four duck species commonly associated with saltwater and oceanic habitats are found with some frequency in winter below dams and on lakes along the Colorado River. One of my favorites is the Long-tailed Duck. These beautiful little ducks breed on ponds in Arctic tundra and then move out into the open ocean. Just about every year, a few migrate into Arizona and overwinter. They like to dive and feed in the deep waters below dams, looking for crustaceans and mollusks. In recent years, Long-tailed Ducks seem to be found more frequently in winter below Glen Canyon Dam, which forms Lake Powell.

Just about every winter, Surf, White-winged, and Black scoters are seen on Lake Havasu. Surf and White-winged are the two that most commonly occur, with Black Scoter being the rarest of the three. These ducks begin arriving in October and often stay around well into March. They can sometimes be found in flocks of up to half a dozen or more birds. Many of these saltwater ducks are females and juveniles that lack the beautiful black body and colored bill of the adult males. Nevertheless, they are a real treat to see.

Of all the waterbirds, Lake Havasu is probably best known for its loons. During the winter months, it is a great place to look for and study these difficult-to-identify waterbirds. Four different loon species have been found on the lake.

The state's first Yellow-billed Loon was found at Painted Rock Reservoir in Maricopa County in 1984. Since that time, there have been several other records, most of which are from Lake Havasu. Yellow-billed Loons are the largest loon of their genus and undoubtedly the rarest in Arizona. Most of them have been seen at or near Site Six, a boat dock area on Lake Havasu not far from the famous London Bridge in Lake Havasu City. Most records are from January and February. Yellow-billed Loons are identified by their large yellowish or straw-colored bill, which appears slightly up-turned. Juveniles often show a distinct auricular patch (a noticeably darker group of feathers on or behind the ear).

Red-throated Loon is Arizona's next-rarest loon and the smallest species of North American loon. They generally migrate into the state in November, with one or two being found just about every winter on Lake Havasu. Red-throated Loons are fairly easy to identify: the best field marks are their small size, light color, and small, slender bill, which is often held at an upturned angle.

Common and Pacific are the two most frequently seen loons on Lake Havasu. They are also the two most difficult to tell apart. Pacific Loons, the rarer of the two species, are seen fairly regularly every winter, sometimes in flocks of up to half a dozen birds. Common Loons are the most commonly occurring loon on the lake. Interestingly, there are summer records of both Common and Pacific loons from Lake Havasu. It appears that one or two Common Loons regularly summer on the lake, and a few Pacific Loons may also summer there from time to time.

Lake Havasu is also a good place to study another group of waterbirds, the grebes. In fact, six different species of grebe have been found on the lake. The most common is the diminutive Pied-billed Grebe. The rarest is the Red-necked, one of the larger North American grebe species. This northern breeder sometimes migrates into Arizona in the winter and is usually found on large bodies of water like Lake Havasu.

Horned Grebe is another northern breeder. Horned Grebes are found regularly every winter on Lake Havasu, sometimes in big numbers. The challenge for birders is trying to separate winter-plumaged Horned Grebes from similar-looking Eared Grebes, which sometimes occur in very large numbers during the winter months.

Lake Havasu is also a very reliable place to see our two largest grebe species, the Western and the very similar-looking Clark's. Though these two look-alike species are often found together, they can also separate themselves from each other, with Clark's being far more numerous in the Bill Williams Delta, and Western being more common on the main body of the lake.

Beginning in September, Lake Havasu regularly attracts a variety of migrating gulls, terns, and jaegers. Mid-September is the time when Sabine's Gulls are regularly found on the lake. These small gulls are easy to spot in flight, showing a striking black, gray-brown, and white wing pattern. In September 2013, the state's first Little Gull was found on Lake Havasu. This species, which breeds in the high Arctic, was long considered overdue in Arizona, as there had been records from just about every other state in the interior West.

September is also the time to look for migrating jaegers, which occasionally visit the state on their fall journey to southern oceans. A few jaegers are found on Lake Havasu just about every September. Of the three jaeger species, Parasitic and Long-tailed are probably the most frequently seen, with Pomarine Jaeger being the rarest. For desert birders with little experience, identifying these Arctic-breeding birds can be a real challenge.

Along with jaegers, watch for migrating terns in September. Both Forster's and Common terns migrate along the Colorado River. Contrary to their name, Common Terns are the more uncommon of the two species. A few Forster's sometimes overwinter on Lake Havasu and can often be spotted in the Bill Williams Delta.

Chapter 1

Many North American gull species breed and summer at high latitudes. That's why you see so few gulls on your summer vacation to the California coast. Each fall, however, many of these northern-breeding gulls withdraw and move south to winter along the Pacific coast, and every year a few find their way to Arizona.

As autumn progresses, gull numbers increase on Colorado River lakes. Ring-billed Gulls occur around Lake Havasu in increasing numbers, with flocks often seen resting along the beach at places like Rotary Park in Lake Havasu and at several of the area's marinas. Occasionally, a Mew Gull is spotted in a flock of Ring-billed Gulls. The Mew Gulls are mostly first-winter birds, and are usually found in mid to late winter. Lake Havasu is also a good place to watch for migrating Bonaparte's Gulls, another northern-breeding species.

November is the time to watch for rare migrating Heermann's Gulls. Unlike gulls that breed in the north and travel south for the winter, these gulls breed in the Gulf of California and move north in the fall to winter along the Pacific coast. From afar and at first glance, they can be mistaken for a jaeger (and vice versa).

In late fall and winter, just about anything can show up along the Colorado River reservoirs. This is the time of year to look for large gulls of the genus *Larus*. The most frequently seen are Herring Gulls, which can sometimes be spotted among resting flocks of Ring-billed Gulls at Rotary Park beach. They can also be found regularly in small numbers around Lake Mohave. Katherine Landing on Lake Mohave is a particularly good gull-watching spot.

Other large gull species that have been seen occasionally in fall and winter at Lake Havasu and other lakes and reservoirs along the Colorado River include Glaucous, Glaucous-winged, Iceland (Thayer's), and Lesser Black-backed. When birding at Lake Havasu in the winter, also keep a lookout for Black-legged Kittiwake, a highly pelagic gull species for which there are a few Arizona and Lake Havasu records.

Undoubtedly the most amazing gull record from the Colorado River is the December 2012 sighting of an Ivory Gull, discovered on a sandbar in the Colorado River about four miles south of Willow Beach below Lake Mohave. Unfortunately, this was a seriously injured bird that probably died not long after its discovery. Ivory Gull is very rarely seen outside its home on ice-packed Arctic seas in the extreme north. Only a few of these birds have been found in the inland western United States.

If an Ivory Gull can show up, who knows what else might find its way to the lakes and reservoirs along the Colorado River in the winter? It's fun to speculate. Among my favorite candidates are Arctic Loon, for which there are winter inland records for the Lower 48 states, and Ancient Murrelet, a small Arctic-breeding alcid, for which there are winter records from large bodies of water in the interior West.

Chapter 1

Special Topic: An Arizona Birder's Calendar

Winter
December

Watch for large *Larus* gulls like Glaucous, Iceland (Thayer's), and Glaucous-winged on reservoirs and lakes, especially along the Colorado River.

Look for wintering species like Cassin's Finch, Rough-legged Hawk, and Northern Shrike in northern Arizona.

Participants on Christmas bird counts often find rare and unusual species, alerting other birders of the opportunity to locate and see them.

January

Wintering waterfowl reach peak numbers on urban lakes and ponds. Look for rare species like Eurasian Wigeon and Greater Scaup.

A great month to go out looking for wintering raptors in central and southeastern Arizona. Try for Ferruginous and Rough-legged hawks, White-tailed Kite, Prairie Falcon, and Merlin.

Check agricultural fields for wintering Sandhill Cranes and occasional Tundra Swans.

February

Search for elusive LeConte's Thrashers, which are singing and beginning to nest.

Look for wintering specialties like Short-eared Owl, Baird's Sparrow, Sprague's Pipit, and Chestnut-collared Longspur in the San Rafael Valley grasslands.

Spring

March

This month sees the onset of spring migration, with a trickle of passage migrants and increasing numbers of returning neotropical nesters. Watch for the return of Cliff Swallows early in the month and Western Kingbirds later in the month.

Common Black-Hawks begin migrating up the Santa Cruz River around the first of the month, reaching peak numbers around March 15.

By the middle of the month, ducks and geese are migrating north in increasing numbers. Check Upper and Lower Lake Mary and Mormon Lake near Flagstaff for migrating waterfowl and wintering Bald Eagles.

April

Spring migration continues to gather strength and nears its peak by month's end. White-winged Doves return to nest in early April. Neotropical-nesting species like Hooded Oriole and Summer Tanager also return this month.

Swainson's Hawks begin migrating through in early April, often in big numbers. Look for them in agricultural areas.

Watch water bodies for migrating Franklin's Gulls and even a rare Heermann's Gull.

Look for shorebirds this month. Check ponds for breeding-plumaged species like Western and Least sandpipers, Dunlin, and Semi-palmated Plover.

Keep an eye out for rare spring-migrating Broad-winged Hawks. Northern Saw-whet Owls begin calling in earnest in the high country.

Townsend's and Hermit warblers begin migrating through higher mountain ranges this month. The six species known as the "Arizona Warblers" (Chapter 3, p.77) return and begin setting up nesting territories toward month's end.

May

Landbird and shorebird migrations reach their peak in the first half of the month and begin to taper off toward the end of the month.

Check small ponds the first week of May for migrating Willets.

May is the third-best month of the year for finding rarities. Check riparian areas for eastern migrants and vagrants.

Slate-throated Redstart, Yellow Grosbeak, and Fan-tailed Warbler are among the very rare Mexican species known to show up in southeastern Arizona in May.

From mid to late May, watch for very rare shorebird species like Hudsonian Godwit and White-rumped Sandpiper at Lake Cochise in southeastern Arizona.

Willow Flycatcher, a late-migrating *Empidonax* flycatcher species, is found toward the end of the month. Endangered Yellow-billed Cuckoos begin arriving in riparian areas like the San Pedro Riparian National Conservation Area at month's end.

Summer

June

In early June, check riparian areas and migrant traps for rare straggling migrants and vagrants.

Common Nighthawks return to northern Arizona. Listen for their "swooshing" courtship sounds at night. Also listen for Flammulated Owls in the pine forests of northern Arizona.

At the end of June, watch for the onset of fall shorebird migration with the arrival of Wilson's Phalarope and Long-billed Curlew. Other Great Basin–breeding birds begin to arrive around this time, including White-faced Ibis and Caspian Tern.

July

Begin to watch for species that disperse from the Gulf of California with the monsoon's onset. They include species like Brown Pelican, Reddish Egret, Little Blue Heron, and Wood Stork.

Rufous Hummingbirds appear around the second week of July, the vanguard of the autumn hummingbird migration.

Fall shorebird migration picks up steam with returning species like Greater and Lesser yellowlegs and an occasional Stilt Sandpiper. Juvenile shorebirds begin arriving in increasing numbers toward the end of the month.

Fall landbird migration begins at the end of July with a trickle of passage migrants, including such species as Western Tanager, Black-headed Grosbeak, and Lazuli Bunting.

August

A good month to watch hummingbirds in southeastern Arizona.

Look for Rivoli's, Blue-throated, Violet-crowned, and an occasional White-eared.

Fall landbird migration continues to build. Watch for Calliope Hummingbirds in northern Arizona and Painted Buntings in southeastern Arizona.

Shorebird migration continues to build toward its peak at the end of the month. Watch for such rare but regularly occurring species as Short-billed Dowitcher and Semipalmated Sandpiper.

Hermit and Townsend's warblers begin migrating through the mountains.

Juvenile Brown Pelicans often arrive from the Gulf of California and can sometimes be found on large and small bodies of water.

Toward the end of the month, many of the "Arizona Warblers" leave Arizona breeding grounds and return to wintering areas in Mexico and Central America.

Fall

September

Fall landbird and shorebird migrations reach their peak early this month and then begin to taper off toward month's end. Check riparian areas and urban areas throughout September for fall migrants.

In the last week of August and first week of September, look for Northern Waterthrushes at small ponds and along streams.

At mid-month, look for migrating Dickcissels around Becker Lake in the White Mountains. Mid-September is also the time to check water bodies for migrating juvenile Sabine's Gulls.

Watch for fall-migrating jaegers, especially on large lakes and reservoirs along the Colorado River.

September is the time to keep a lookout for White-fronted Geese arriving from their summer Arctic breeding grounds.

Broad-winged Hawks can be seen at Yaki Point during the height of fall raptor migration, with the best time to see one around September 29.

October

Fall landbird migration begins to wind down, but the first half of October is an excellent time to look for rare eastern migrants and vagrants. Wintering sparrows and blackbirds begin to arrive. Watch for returning Brewer's Blackbirds. Check flocks of Brewer's and Chipping sparrows for an occasional Clay-colored Sparrow.

This is a good month to look for more uncommon and rare shorebirds like Pectoral Sandpiper, Sanderling, American Golden-Plover, and Ruff.

At the end of the month, keep an eye out for migrating scoters.

November

This month sees the influx of wintering landbirds and waterbirds. Toward the end of the month, check large bodies of water—especially the lakes and reservoirs along the Colorado River—for winter visitors like scoters, Red-throated and Pacific loons, and Red-necked and Horned grebes. Check below Parker Dam for Barrow's Goldeneye.

Watch larger water bodies for migrating Heermann's and Bonaparte's gulls.

Chapter 2: Identifying Birds

Ways to improve your bird-finding and identification skills are discussed in this chapter. "Beginning with the Basics" offers some practical hints and suggestions that will help beginning birders get started. Then we move beyond basics and discuss some specific strategies that will help you better identify birds. "Listening to Birds" discusses why it's important to learn and memorize birdsongs and calls, something I always emphasize on field trips. To suggest some techniques and methods for doing so, I'll take you along on a visit to Madera Canyon, one of the state's best places to hear owls and nightjars and listen for such sought-after species as Elegant Trogon, Sulfur-bellied Flycatcher, and Arizona Woodpecker. "Looking at Beaks" explains how careful examination of beaks can be a valuable aid in helping you correctly identify some of Arizona's more hard-to-identify birds, especially among the passerines and shorebirds. At the end of this chapter is a list of suggested books, magazines, and online resources for beginning birders.

Beginning with the Basics

Birding is a fun and challenging pursuit just about anyone can enjoy. All that's required to start out are an interest in birds, a pair of binoculars, and a field guide. With these tools and a little outdoor experience, you can begin a lifelong interest in learning about birds.

Birding Arizona

Before You Go

A good day of birding requires both luck and preparation. The day before, take some time to go through a field guide and a checklist for your target area, if available, to familiarize yourself with bird species you're likely to encounter or particular species you hope to find. That way, you'll have a mental picture of what the bird looks like and can concentrate on watching it when you see it, instead of fumbling through a guidebook or trying to bring up a photograph of the bird on a phone or tablet.

For example, before starting out to look for migrating birds in the fall, I spend time with field guides, reviewing hard-to-identify birds or groups of birds I'm likely to encounter, such as the flycatchers and fall-plumaged warblers and sparrows. It's particularly useful to brush up on shorebird identification before the onset of their fall migration. The same thing holds true when looking for species you're likely to first locate by voice. If, for example, you are searching for grassland species like Cassin's, Botteri's, and Grasshopper sparrows, it's very helpful to listen to recording of their songs before setting out.

Most birding field guides are comprehensive. They have illustrations or photographs of hundreds of species and cover large geographic areas. For beginning birders, this can be quite intimidating. To make things easier, some guides have editions that cover smaller geographic areas. Some local Audubon Societies, such as those in Maricopa County, Tucson, and northern Arizona, publish field guides to their areas. You can also limit or pare down the number of species to look through by using birding checklists and the online eBird program. Checklists and eBird provide information about the abundance and seasonal status of birds in a specific area. They'll give you an idea of which birds are common in that area, which you can then look up in the field guide so you'll recognize them by sight. Be aware that many birds molt or grow distinct and different feathers (plumages) depending on their age and the time of year. Field guides will show you these differences.

When planning your outing, keep an eye on the weather. Strong weather systems can be a birder's ally. Storms sometimes bring in rare and unusual species. They can even cause a so-called bird "fallout." Tropical storms moving up from the Gulf of California in the summer and powerful winter storms from the Pacific Ocean can carry unusual birds into Arizona. This can even happen with more localized weather disturbances like summer "chubascos" (summer rainstorms) and heavy winter snowstorms in northern Arizona.

So, what time of day should you go birding? Passerines (perching birds) are usually more active and easier to see and hear early in the morning. They tend to become less active as the day progresses, especially during the midday heat. There is often another spurt of activity later in the afternoon. This does not mean you always need to get out birding right at the crack of dawn. Birds often don't move around until it warms up and insects become active, especially during the colder winter months. Many raptors (hawks, falcons, and vultures) do not begin flying and soaring until the morning air has warmed enough to give them lift. Like us, birds are creatures of habit, with cyclic patterns of activity. If you see a bird at a particular time of day and want to see it again, try returning to that location at the same time the next day.

Birding Arizona

Birders are often advised not to wear brightly colored or white clothing when birding. I have never found this to be a particular problem, but it's probably sound advice, especially when searching for very shy species in a situation where bright or white colors might tend to magnify your movement.

There's one final thing to do so you're ready to go birding: invest in a good pair of binoculars. For birders, they're indispensable. I often tell people that when you go out for a day of birding, you can forget anything (lunch, jacket, and sunscreen) except the binoculars. Before you decide what to buy, do some online research, talk to other birders, and try out several pairs. Good binoculars can be purchased at a reasonable cost. Once you have them, you're ready for the field.

In the Field

The secret to finding birds is the habitat. Different birds like different habitats. To find the habitats that are most likely to attract birds, it's useful to learn to identify some common plants and trees. Birds are often found feeding on species like mulberry, hackberry, juniper, Russian olive, chokecherry, and pyracantha. One spring morning, I watched a beautiful assortment of Western Tanagers, Cedar Waxwings, and Black-headed Grosbeaks all feeding in a single fruiting mulberry tree at Cameron Trading Post in northern Arizona. Tube-shaped flowers such as gilia and penstemon are famous for attracting hummingbirds. Look for acorn-loving species like woodpeckers, jays, and wild turkeys in areas with oak trees. At Boyce Thompson Arboretum near Superior, fruiting Chinese pistachio trees are a magnet for birds in autumn. Over the years, such rare species as Rufous-backed Robin and Varied Thrush have been found feasting on the trees' blue-colored berries.

When you encounter a lot of bird activity, stay put and look at the birds. The urge to move on in an effort to find more birds can be powerful, but try to ignore it, at least for a little while. When you find a flock of birds moving across the landscape, though, follow it and give attention to each member of the flock. Some flocks, called "mixed flocks," include several different species.

As you bird, be sure to obey "no trespassing" signs. Arizona has extensive private ranch and agricultural lands, as well as tribal lands that are good birding locations. Make it a general rule to ask permission, whenever possible, to bird in these areas. It's always advisable to explain why you're there and what you are doing.

Nothing is more difficult and frustrating than trying to watch a bird as you face into the glare of sunlight, so pay attention to the sun. Whenever possible, search with the sun to your back. This is especially important when trying to spot birds through a spotting scope as you investigate a large body of water like Lake Havasu.

What should you do when you spot a bird but only get a fleeting glimpse before it flies off or disappears into dense foliage? Birders who take time to methodically search an area can often relocate the bird and get better looks. When birds fly away, they often fly only a short distance. Sometimes, they even return to the area where they were originally observed. Searching in ever-widening circles or patiently waiting and listening in the area are all good techniques if you want to relocate your target bird.

When birding, we tend to keep our eyes focused ahead or

up in the trees. Don't forget to look up into the sky. Hawks, eagles, and swifts often fly and soar high overhead and can easily be overlooked if you don't look up and scan the sky from time to time.

Always have a field guide with you for consultation. However, when you see a bird you can't identify, try to stay focused on the bird. Don't take your eyes off and rush to look for a matching bird in your field guide. Instead, take time to carefully observe the bird, making mental notes of as many identifying field marks as you can. Later, go back and look it up in your field guide. If you like to take pictures, try to get a photograph, particularly if it is a rare species, but don't be so anxious to get a photograph that you fail to take a good look at the bird first. If it flies away before you look, you might not end up with a decent photograph anyway, and you will have missed critical field marks.

Don't worry if you make an identification mistake. There's not an experienced birder alive who has not misidentified a bird on occasion.

Attracting Birds

Birders rely more and more on electronic devices to play or record and play back birdsongs in the field. This is a very effective way of attracting target species. Like any good thing, however, it can be overdone. And, of course, it can be abused. Song recordings should be used judiciously. They can be particularly disruptive to nesting birds, which need to spend their limited energy reserves tending their young instead of responding to recordings. Recordings should never be used around hawk and owl nests. With two of our endangered owl species, Mexican Spotted Owl and Ferruginous

Pygmy-Owl, the use of recording is against the law. Pounding on the trunks of trees to try to get owls to look out of their nest holes should never be done.

The more traditional technique the birding community uses for attracting birds is "pishing," making a noise that sounds something like the hissing sound made at a villain in a movie. It can be a very effective way to get birds to come into view where they can be observed. There are several theories as to why the sound attracts birds. One is that it resembles alarm calls of birds that come together in flocks to chase away predators. Another is that the sound resembles the one made by a bird that has been captured by a predator, prompting other birds to fly in and investigate.

Whatever the reason, pishing often works. It can be particularly effective at higher elevations in Arizona for attracting species like chickadees, nuthatches, titmice, and warblers. Pishing even works for shorebirds. I have a friend, a master "pisher", who can coax in shorebird species like Western, Least, and Baird's sandpipers. However, it can also backfire and chase them away. Interestingly, "pishing" does not seem to work in tropical forests. I've tried to get small birds in the Peruvian Amazon to respond to my pishing, without success.

Because your goal is to lure birds in for a closer look, keep your movements small and slow. Sudden movements frighten birds. When you're birding with other birders, don't make a sudden motion with your arm to point out a bird. More often than not, the movement will scare it away. Learn to verbally describe the location of a bird for other birders.

On the other hand, you can use arm movements to your

advantage. Sometimes, you need to get a bird or group of birds to fly to confirm an identification. If you're looking at a distant group of gulls, for example, and want to get them airborne, try vigorously flapping your arms up and down. This technique will almost always cause your target bird to take flight.

Never Stop Learning

Get in the habit of keeping a list of the birds you see. Sightings of rare birds should be reported to the Arizona Bird Committee, to alert other birders and to increase our knowledge of Arizona's birdlife. Whenever possible, try to get photographs of rare and unusual species and submit them to the committee along with a written description. You can also submit photographs to the Arizona Field Ornithologists. They keep a photographic archive of rare and unusual Arizona birds on their website.

If you're a new birder, make a point of going on field trips and guided bird walks. It's a wonderful way to meet other birders and learn about new places to watch birds. These trips are usually led by experienced birders who can help you with information and techniques that will improve your identification skills … skills it can take a lifetime to hone.

Listening to Birds

It's no secret that the best birders do much of their birding by ear. As a beginning birder, I was always amazed watching experienced birders who could accurately identify several different species singing at the same time. Identifying birds by sound is always a challenge. Most birders are visual learners who start out identifying birds by sight. Only after they have substantial experience with visual identification do they begin learning bird sounds. However, learning and memorizing the songs and calls of birds is well worth the time and effort.

There are many reasons to learn birdsongs. First and foremost, knowing them helps us locate birds. As a birder, you often hear birds before you see them. The time spent at home learning their songs not only helps you locate common species but can sometimes lead to the discovery of a rare and unusual bird whose song might otherwise have been overlooked, ignored, or simply dismissed as a variant of the song of a more common bird. Several very rare Mexican species, such as the Sinaloa Wren, Fan-tailed Warbler, and the first US record of Pine Flycatcher, have initially been located and identified by birders familiar with their calls and songs.

Some common species are almost always easier to hear than see, often because of the type of habitat they occupy. In southeastern Arizona, for example, Cassin's and Botteri's sparrows are easy to find by voice but often remain very difficult to see in their tall grassland habitat.

Some bird species are so similar in appearance that voice identification is the easiest and surest way to tell them apart. The call notes of Long-billed and Short-billed dowitchers are one of the most reliable ways to identify and separate these two look-alike shorebirds, which often occur together in autumn. Western and Eastern meadowlarks are found together in parts of Arizona. The easiest way to tell these two apart is by their very distinctive and different songs and calls. In the case of two identical-looking *Empidonax* flycatchers, Cordilleran and Pacific-slope, the only way to separate them in the field is by voice. Very rare sightings of Couch's Kingbird, Eastern Wood-Pewee, and Nutting's Flycatcher often require voice confirmation to separate them from the more common and expected Tropical Kingbird, Western Wood-Pewee, and Ash-throated Flycatcher.

There are many other examples where voice is helpful in separating similar-looking species. Some of them include distinguishing Downy Woodpecker from Hairy Woodpecker, Black-capped Chickadee from Mountain Chickadee, Common Raven from American Crow, Greater Yellowlegs from Lesser Yellowlegs, Black-tailed Gnatcatcher from Black-capped Gnatcatcher, and Common Nighthawk from Lesser Nighthawk. Knowing the call notes and songs of Buff-breasted, Dusky, Gray, Hammond's, and Willow flycatchers can be a great aid in identifying these hard-to-identify flycatchers. Knowing call notes can also help identify confusing look-alike shorebirds such as Baird's, Least, and Western sandpipers.

On the other hand, species that do not necessarily look alike can have very similar songs and calls. You cannot always assume that the voice you hear belongs to the bird you think it does. For example, the calls of Brown Creeper and Golden-crowned Kinglet sound alike, and these two species can occupy very similar habitat. The Broad-billed Hummingbird has a call that sounds to me much like the call of the Ruby-crowned Kinglet. Red-faced and Yellow warblers have very similar-sounding songs, as do Black-headed Grosbeak and Hepatic Tanager. Two of our hawk species, Red-tailed and Swainson's, have sound-alike calls. The call note of a

Green-tailed Towhee can be confused with the catlike call of the Gray Catbird. The "chuck" call of the Hermit Thrush can be confused with similar calls made by the Hepatic Tanager and the Fox Sparrow. You might confuse the alarm call of a Gunnison's Prairie Dog with a Cooper's or Sharp-shinned hawk. The call notes of Northern Cardinal and Pyrrhuloxia are very much alike, but if you listen closely, the cardinal's is a sharp "chip"-like note, while the Pyrrhuloxia's is a flatter note often followed by a sputtered "tttsk." One of the most frequent errors I make in the field is mistaking the "chip" note of a Northern Cardinal for a warbler species.

Then there are the mimics—birds that copy and imitate the songs of other birds. Northern Mockingbirds are a famous example. I once listened to a mockingbird in Tucson rattle off in rapid succession the songs of about seven other desert-dwelling species. On another occasion, I was birding in the northeastern part of the state near Tuba City and found a Northern Mockingbird imitating the songs of a Verdin and a Curve-billed Thrasher, neither of which occur in the area. It told me that not only was the mockingbird an excellent mimic, but it must have grown up in or traveled to other parts of the state. Another mockingbird near Ganado Lake insisted on repeating in succession the calls of Woodhouse's Scrub Jay followed by those of Pinyon Jay.

A bird many people do not associate with mimicry is the Lesser Goldfinch. These tiny finches can mimic many other species, including American Kestrel, Ash-throated Flycatcher, Black-chinned Hummingbird, and Say's Phoebe, to name just a few. Steller's Jays are another mimic and are well-known for imitating the call of Red-tailed Hawks. When you hear a Red-tailed Hawk call, particularly when birding at higher elevations, be suspicious.

Birding Arizona

It just might be an imitation performed by a Steller's Jay.

Besides songs and calls, some bird species have evolved song substitutes to use in place of songs to attract mates and defend territories. On summer evenings in northern Arizona, you can sometimes hear the display dives of Common Nighthawks. This sound is made by air rushing through the birds' wing feathers, creating a booming or swooshing noise at the bottom of the dive. One of my favorite song substitutes is made by the male Broad-tailed Hummingbird. As it flies through the forest, this humming-bird makes a loud, insect-like trill that's often described as a police whistle. This sound is caused by the hummingbird's primary feathers.

Woodpeckers announce their territory and attract mates by using their pointed, chisel-like bill to drum on trees and cacti. Some people say they can differentiate woodpecker species by noting the difference in rhythm and cadence of the drumming. I've never had much success at this, although there are a couple of exceptions. The American Three-toed Woodpecker has a short drum that makes a hollow "bonk bonk" sound. This drum starts out slowly, accelerates, and then decelerates. You can often hear this sound in the high country, especially in springtime. The drumming of sapsuckers is also fairly easy to recognize. It's a loud burst of banging followed by slowly decreasing and irregular tapping. The quality of sound produced by woodpeckers greatly depends, of course, on the type of substrate the bird is pounding on.

Doves and pigeons can often be identified by the sound their wings make when they fly. Mourning Doves make a diagnostic whistling sound. Inca Doves make a distinct and easy-to-identify rattling noise with their wings as they flush. You often hear Band-tailed Pigeons before you catch sight of them. These large pigeons make a distinctive "whap whap whap" sound with their wings as they fly off their perches.

Many of us have our favorite way of learning and remembering birdsongs. Of course, with the name-sayers—birds named after the sound of their song or call—the job is fairly easy. With more difficult songs and calls, there are a variety of other techniques that can help. They include phonetic representation, such as the "who cooks for you" song of the White-winged Dove; comparative ideas, like the "tin trumpet" song of a Red-breasted Nuthatch; and even descriptive words, such as the "flute-like" song of a Hermit Thrush.

Over the years, with the help of birding friends, I have gathered a list of phonetic representations and other ways to help me learn and remember the songs and calls of several Arizona bird species.

 A few of my favorites:

Scaled Quail:
Sounds like he is saying,
"chump change; chump change"

Montezuma Quail:
A descending call that reminds me of the sound made by
Wile E. Coyote as he falls off a cliff toward the desert floor in
Road Runner cartoons

Birding Arizona

Inca Dove:
Gives a distinctive call
"no hope, no hope"

Northern Saw-whet Owl:
Sounds like a ship at sea sending a wireless message

Mexican Jay:
Tells the rest of the flock to *"wait, wait"*

Greater Pewee:
Says *"Jose Maria"*

Brown-crested Flycatcher:
Listen and you may hear,
"What! What!" "Beer! Beer!" "Where is it? Where is it?"

Dusky-capped Flycatcher:
A mournful *"pee-ur"*

Sulfur-bellied Flycatcher:
Sounds like the squeeking of a child's rubber duck

Cassin's Kingbird:
Loudly calls out *"Come here"* or *"Come ear"*

Bewick's Wren:
Sounds like the dial return of an old rotary telephone

Thick-billed Kingbird:
Gives a loud, head-turning, up-slurred *"zureet"*

Chapter 2

Western Kingbird:
Sounds like the fast-forwarding of a tape recorder

Cactus Wren:
Sounds like a car motor turning over, *"chug chug chug"*

Bell's Vireo:
Asks himself a question, then gives himself the answer; for instance,
"Which way to Wichita?" and then *"This way to Wichita."*

Curve-billed Thrasher:
Gives a distinctive call *"whip, whip"*

Madera Canyon in the Santa Rita Mountains in southeastern Arizona is a fun place to learn birdsongs, especially at night. Besides being home to several fairly easy-to-find owl species, Madera Canyon is also a good place to hear other night birds, including three nightjars that are famous name-sayers.

On summer evenings, Mexican Whip-poor-wills usually begin giving their namesake calls shortly after dusk. Another namesake nightjar, the Common Poorwill, can often be heard in the same area up on the rocky slopes that flank the canyon. Every few years, a rare Mexican species is found in the drier lower reaches of Madera Canyon: the Buff-collared Nightjar. It is another name-sayer, but it gives its name in Spanish. Its distinctive song is phonetically represented in Spanish as *prestame tu cuchillo*, which translates into "Lend me your knife." It's fun to imagine how the name may have come about as two or three Mexican vaqueros were sitting around a campfire eating dinner at nightfall, listening to the bird off in the distance.

If listening to and learning the songs of night birds is insufficient challenge, the Madera Canyon area has lots of other birds that will test your birdsong identification skills. I particularly remember one summer morning shortly after dawn, hiking up the trial that leads out of the Bog Springs Campground. As the trail crossed through a beautiful grove of sycamores, silverleaf oaks, and pines, an incredible dawn chorus of songs began, all of which sounded very much alike.

Unraveling that confusing medley of sound took a pleasant hour. The sound-alike birds responsible were Hepatic and Western tanagers, Black-headed Grosbeaks, and American Robins, with a Warbling Vireo or two thrown in for good measure. Toward the end of the hike, one of the area's most famous summering birds began giving its turkey-like, croaking call. Yes, it was an Elegant Trogon. A little farther down the trail came a loud "peek" call belonging to one of the *Dryobates* woodpeckers. I didn't find the caller, so I finished the hike wondering was it an Arizona or a Hairy.

Another very challenging place to test your birdsong identification skills is a marsh. These watery areas with their dense cattails and bulrushes can harbor a variety of interesting birds. When you visit them, however, you're often confronted by a chorus of strange and unfamiliar sounds. A variety of marsh inhabitants are responsible for this jumble of clucks, ticks, buzzes, and rattles, including rails, herons, grebes, yellowthroats, and those noisy marsh residents, the Marsh Wren and Red-winged Blackbird—not to mention frogs and insects.

Many marsh birds are notoriously hard to see, staying hidden from sight, allowing only occasional glimpses as they slip in and out of dense vegetation. With the rails, for example, you rarely get to see them, but if you listen carefully, you can often hear their distinctive songs and calls. Most rails have varied repertoires, and birders should be familiar with these variations. This is the case with Arizona's two large rails, Virginia Rail and the recently split Ridgeway's Rail. The springtime breeding song of the Virginia Rail is an easily recognized and learned series of "kid dic kid dic" notes. This rail also gives several pig-like grunts. Among the calls given by Ridgeway's Rail is a series of fast-paced "yak yak yak" sounds that remind me of a car engine turning over. Another call is a series of harsh, raspy "kek kek kek" sounds. The Sora gives a squealing whinny-like song that descends toward the end. Sometimes, however, the Sora is content to keep repeating only the first note.

One of my very favorite rail songs is that of the Black Rail, which in Arizona is only found in marshes along the Colorado River. Black Rails have an unmistakable call that cannot be confused with the utterance of any other marsh inhabitant. It is a loud "kiki-doo" that is generally heard early in the morning or in the evening. Trying to see one of these tiny rails, however, is another matter. On a field trip to Mittry Lake near Yuma to look for Black Rails, the group spotted one almost by chance virtually frozen in a tiny opening at the base of thick bulrushes. It was so perfectly still and so well hidden that some of the participants never were able to spot it through their binoculars.

Two marsh residents, Common Gallinule and American

Coot, are fairly easy to see and identify. At times, however, they hide out in dense emergent vegetation. This is especially true of the Common Gallinule, which seems to be the shyer species. These two birds have very similar calls, and it's always a challenge to try to separate them by voice alone. The gallinule's voice has a very nasal, questioning quality, while the coot's voice is harsher and more complaining.

When birding in marshes, if you hear a call you don't recognize, it is very often a Red-winged Blackbird. I'm always amazed at the number and variety of whistles, clucks, and gurgles made by this marsh-breeding species.

Take time to learn and memorize birdsongs and calls. It will greatly add to your birding pleasure and enhance your ability to find and correctly identify bird species. There is a wealth of recordings, available on disc or via online resources like xeno-canto, that can be used to aid learning. In addition, the Arizona Field Ornithologists host a sound library on their website with recordings of a number of Arizona bird species.

Looking at Beaks

A number of Arizona bird species present difficult identification challenges, especially for beginning birders. After all, many bird species look alike, and plumage differences are often not that helpful. Bird's beaks can be one of the most important field marks used by birders to separate many look-alike and hard-to-identify species.

When I was a beginning birder, four Arizona species in

particular often gave me trouble: Greater Yellowlegs from Lesser Yellowlegs, and Ash-throated Flycatcher from Brown-crested Flycatcher. Focusing on these species' beaks allowed me to confidently separate them in the field when they were not vocalizing. In the case of the Greater Yellowlegs, I learned to look for its longer, slightly upturned beak as opposed to the straighter beak of the Lesser Yellowlegs, which is only slightly longer than the diameter of its head. With the two flycatchers, it was noting the long, almost snout-like beak of the Brown-crested Flycatcher as opposed to the noticeably shorter beak of the Ash-throated.

There are many other examples where beak size is the best field mark for separating difficult look-alike species. The small, dainty beak of the Downy Woodpecker—which is only about as long as one-third the diameter of its head, or less—is the best way to separate it from the Hairy Woodpecker. In winter, an occasional Ross's Goose is sometimes spotted in flocks of similar-looking Snow Geese. The short, stubby beak of the Ross's is a reliable aid in differentiating it from the Snow Goose, with its much longer beak. The thin, squashed-down beak of a female Red-breasted Merganser can help separate it from the female Common Merganser. Noting the very long and relatively thick beak of the Tropical Kingbird is a good way to tell it at a glance from Western and Cassin's kingbirds, both of which have a much shorter beak. The thinner, straighter beak of the Pacific Loon helps distinguish it from the Common Loon, with its thicker and more angled beak, and the larger beak of Botteri's Sparrow is useful in separating it from a similar-looking grassland species, the Cassin's Sparrow. Beak size can also be a valuable aid in separating American Crow and Common Raven in areas in Arizona where their ranges overlap.

Birding Arizona

Every summer, I like to take some time to read and brush up on my shorebird identifications. In a few weeks, I'll be confronted with a host of juvenile and basic-plumaged shorebirds to sort through and identify. Familiarity with the sizes and shapes of beaks is often the key to identifying these Arctic-breeding migrants. The Dunlin, Stilt and Western sandpipers all have noticeably curved or drooping beaks. In fact, the length and curvature of the Western Sandpiper's beak is one of the best ways of separating it from the very similar Semipalmated Sandpiper, which migrates through Arizona in small numbers each fall. Carefully noting beak length and thickness is important in separating other basic-plumaged shorebird species, like American Golden-Plover from Black-bellied Plover, and Red Phalarope from Red-necked Phalarope.

Experienced birders know that beak shape and size can be critical in correctly identifying many rare and vagrant species. This is often the case with the gulls and terns, two groups with which Arizona birders often have little experience. When you're scoping through a flock of first-winter Ring-billed Gulls, beak size and shape are important clues in spotting an occasional first-winter Mew Gull, whose beak is subtly thinner than that of the Ring-billed. The longer, slightly drooping beak of a Laughing Gull is a very helpful aid in separating that rare vagrant from the more commonly occurring Franklin's Gull. Likewise, the drooping beak of the Elegant Tern is one of the surest ways of distinguishing it from other tern species, including the even rarer Royal Tern. The longer beaks of Red-eyed and Yellow-green vireos are a good way to help separate them from other confusing vireo species such as Warbling and Philadelphia. Finally, the small, stubby beak of the

Cackling Goose is one of the best field marks for separating it from the various races of the Canada Goose.

In addition to size and shape, beak color can also be a very useful field mark. However, it must be used with caution. Beak color can vary with the season and age of the bird, and there can be substantial variation among individuals. Color also depends on the amount of light hitting the bill (another word for beak). At Lake Pleasant, I once spotted what at first appeared to be a very rare Yellow-billed Loon. However, it turned out to be a Common Loon. Morning sunlight striking the Common Loon's grayish bill had made it appear yellow.

A few obvious examples where beak color is an important field mark are the bicolored beak of a juvenile Glaucous Gull, the yellow beak of an adult Least Tern, the straw- or yellowish-colored beak of a Yellow-billed Loon, and the red bill of a Broad-billed Hummingbird. There are many examples where more subtle differences in beak color can aid in identification. For example, the black-tipped lower mandible of a Gray Flycatcher can help separate it from the other small *Empidonax* flycatchers. Often overlooked is the subtly white-tipped bill of the Horned Grebe, which can be used to distinguish it from the Eared Grebe when these two species are in basic plumage. Another often-overlooked color field mark is the bicolored bill of the Northern Parula. This is especially helpful when looking at one of these active birds flitting about in branches high overhead.

Careful examination of beak size and color can also help birders identify races or subspecies of birds. Many birders keep track of subspecies, knowing that someday they may be split into a separate species and can thus be added to a "life list" (a record a birder keeps of species seen over the years or during a lifetime.)

Two very similar races of the Dark-eyed Junco, the Gray-headed and the Red-backed, can be found in Arizona. These two junco races have almost identical plumage, with their reddish back being one of the most obvious field marks. Careful birders are able to separate the two based mostly on the color of the beak, which is bicolored flesh-and-black in the Red-backed, and all flesh-colored in the Gray-headed. Another species that, like the Dark-eyed Junco, is undergoing obvious and rapid speciation is the Fox Sparrow. Four different races of the Fox Sparrow have been found in Arizona in the winter. The rarest is the Thick-billed form, which breeds in California. It can easily be distinguished from the other races, including the more commonly occurring Slate-colored form, by its very large beak.

Looking at beaks not only helps us identify birds, but it can also teach us much about how birds have evolved. One of the things birding gives us is a window into the evolutionary processes that shape the natural world. It was, after all, his observations of birds that formed much of the basis of Charles Darwin's theory of biological evolution. Birders are, likewise, uniquely situated to observe firsthand many of these biological processes. Looking at the beaks of birds can be especially instructive.

As we have seen, beaks are one of the most prominent and observable features of birds. These hard, bony structures are a heritable trait passed down from generation to generation. Evolution through natural selection has shaped and molded them in many different ways. One of the important things we can learn from studying bird's beaks is that natural selection is not necessarily an imperceptible step-by-step process that takes tens of thousands or millions of years. In fact, it can happen almost before our very eyes. That's one of the lessons of the finches' beaks studied in depth and detail by Peter Grant and written about by Jonathan Weiner in his book *The Beak of the Finch*. Grant and his colleagues could actually measure changes in beak size of finches in the Galapagos as the birds responded to selective pressures like drought and competition from other species.

The beaks of Red Crossbills, a wide-ranging North American finch species, offer another insight into evolutionary processes. Red Crossbills breed in Arizona's conifer forests. Feeding in spruce and fir trees, they sometimes hang upside down on cones, using their beak to extract seeds. Seen up close, the beak actually looks deformed, with the upper and lower mandibles completely crossing over one another. This bizarre-looking beak enables these birds to pry open and extract seeds from tightly closed cones they would otherwise be unable to open.

Craig W. Beckman and Anna K. Lindholm are two Canadian researchers who performed an interesting experiment on Red Crossbills. They straightened the crossbills' beaks by clipping them, making it impossible for the birds to pry open their usual cones. As the beak slowly grew back—much like our fingernails do—the twist in the beak reappeared and slowly became more pronounced. It was, in effect, a way of mimicking the evolution of the beak. As this continued, the birds were gradually able to open more and more difficult cones until the beaks finally grew back completely, allowing them to once again open their accustomed cones. The experiment demonstrated that even a small mutation like a slight twist in the beak can confer a selective advantage that can become more pronounced through successive generations, opening up an entirely new food niche.

Through mutation and natural selection, the beaks of birds have evolved into a variety of different shapes and sizes that allow them to be used in many different ways. Hawks and falcons have evolved sharp, hooked beaks that allow them to rip and tear into prey. Mergansers have long, serrated bills that help them seize and hold fish. Woodpeckers have long, stout beaks with chisel-like points that they use to excavate nest cavities and peel off tree bark in search of beetles and other insects. Herons and other wading birds have evolved daggerlike bills that allow them to spear fish and amphibians. Evolution has produced a variety of beak sizes and shapes that allow birds to eat seeds. These range from the tiny seed-cracking beaks of goldfinches and sparrows to the massive nutcracker-like jaws of Evening Grosbeaks and Northern Cardinals. Brown and White pelicans use their huge, net-like beaks to catch fish, and hummingbirds have thin, needle-like beaks that allow them to sip nectar from deep in the tubular blossoms of flowers.

One of my favorite birding pastimes is watching shorebirds feed along the muddy edges of lakes and ponds. Many of these highly migratory birds have evolved tube-shaped beaks that they use to probe into the sand or mud in search of a variety of small worms and other invertebrates. Shorebird beaks come in many sizes, lengths, and shapes. This allows the birds to probe and feed at different depths and in different niches as they wade or sometimes swim in the water. The phalaropes often spin in circles, daintily picking food from near the water's surface with long, thin beaks. Long-billed Dowitchers move their long, tubular bill up and down with sewing machine–like precision, probing deeply into the mud. Semipalmated Plovers do not probe but find food visually, then pluck it from near the surface with their small bill. Perhaps no shorebird bill is more spectacular than the long, recurved bill of the American Avocet. These beautiful shorebirds often capture food by sweeping their upturned bill back and forth through the water.

Several summers ago on a trip to northern Arizona, I thought it might be fun to stop and look at the famous dinosaur tracks that can be seen in a rocky outcropping not far off US Route 160 near Tuba City. As I looked at those footprints frozen in the red sandstone of the Mesozoic era, two Common Ravens flew in and began hopping about on the rocks. It was a somewhat curious but very appropriate juxtaposition. It's believed that modern-day birds evolved from a lineage of theropod dinosaurs that date from approximately the same time period as the bipedal dinosaurs that left their footprints in that mud over 200 million years ago. Birds' nearest relatives, the dinosaurs, are long extinct. The birds, however, have traveled on and evolved in a wondrous variety of ways. Watching birds, and looking carefully at their beaks, can not only help us identify them, but give us unique insights into and appreciation for some of the evolutionary processes that made their long journey possible.

Birding Arizona

Special Topic:
Suggested Books and Online Resources for Beginning Birders

Bird Identification Guides:

Kaufman, Kenn. 2005. *Field Guide to the Birds of North America*. New York: Houghton Mifflin. (This has over 900 digitized photographs of the birds of North America.)

Sibley, David. 2014. *The Sibley Guide to Birds, Second Edition*. New York: Alfred A. Knopf. (This has over 900 illustrations covering the birds of North America. A smaller edition covers just the birds of western North America.)

The National Geographic Society. 2017. *Field Guide to the Birds of North America*. Washington D.C.: National Geographic. (This has illustrations of over 1,000 North American species.)

Guides to Arizona Birding Locations and General Reference:

Brandt, Frank and Linda. 2001. *Birding the Flagstaff Area*. Sedona: Northern Arizona Audubon Society.

Burns, Jim. 2008. *Arizona Birds: from Backyard to the Backwoods*. Tucson: Univ. of Arizona Press.

Corman, Troy E., and Catherine Wise-Gervais. 2005. *Arizona Breeding Bird Atlas*. Albuquerque: Univ. of New Mexico Press.

Sibley, David A. 2002. *Sibley's Birding Basics*. New York: Alfred A. Knopf.

Stejskal, David, and Gary H. Rosenberg, compilers. 2011. *Finding Birds in Southeastern Arizona*. Tucson: Tucson Audubon Society.

Taylor, Richard. 2005. *A Birder's Guide to Southeastern Arizona*. Delaware City: American Birding Association.

Taylor, Richard. 2017. *Birds of Southeastern Arizona*. Olympia: RW Morse Company.

Witzeman, Janet L., and Troy Corman. 2017. *Birds of Phoenix and Maricopa County Arizona*. Phoenix: Maricopa Audubon Society.

Magazines:

Bird Watcher's Digest, published by Pardson Corporation

Birding, published by the American Birding Association

BirdWatching, published by Rick Kessel

Online Resources:

Arizona Bird Committee, http://abc.azfo.org/

Arizona Field Ornithologists, http://www.azfo.org/

Audubon and Cornell Lab of Ornithology's eBird program, http://ebird.org

xeno-canto (for birdsongs), http://www.xeno-canto.org

Chapter 3: Some Special Arizona Birds

Most birders are familiar with such well-known south-eastern Arizona species as Elegant Trogon, Rose-throated Becard, Rivoli's and Blue-throated hummingbirds, and Varied Bunting. In this chapter, you will be introduced to several less famous but equally interesting Arizona bird species. They include six beautiful summer residents I call the "Arizona Warblers," two highly specialized and fascinating northern Arizona species (Pinyon Jay and Clark's Nutcracker), and all of Arizona's woodpeckers and wrens. In "Watching Hawks," you'll read about several unique raptors seen at spring and fall hawk-watching sites along the Santa Cruz River and at the Grand Canyon. This chapter concludes with suggestions for when to look for rare and unusual species.

The Arizona Warblers

Of the 51 small, colorful songbirds known as warblers found in the Lower 48 states, most occur from the Great Plains east. About a dozen are scattered across the western and southwestern states, but they are not distributed evenly. In fact, only Arizona can lay claim to having a large or significant portion of the breeding ranges of six of the species. These "Arizona Warblers," as I like to call them, are the Grace's, Lucy's, Red-faced, Olive, and Virginia's warblers, and the Painted Redstart. They're not the only warblers that breed in Arizona, of course, but they form a unique and intriguing group.

Birding Arizona

Three of the six—Red-faced and Virginia's warblers, along with Painted Redstart—build their nests on the ground, and Lucy's is almost singular among warblers for its preference for nesting in tree cavities. Only two of the six are closely related: Lucy's and Virginia's are members of the genus *Oreothlypis*. Taxonomists place one species, Olive Warbler, in its own family due to its uncertain relationship with other species. Grace's, Lucy's, and Virginia's, all named in honor of family members of 19th-century naturalists, are the only North American songbirds named for women. The best thing about these species, however, is that all six can often be found close to one another in easily accessible mountain ranges in central and southeastern Arizona.

I enjoy looking for these warblers every spring. By late April, most have arrived on their breeding grounds and are singing in territories. It's helpful to review their songs before setting out. Several can be mistaken for the songs of other warbler species, and Olive Warblers can be confusing because they sound more like bluebirds and titmice than warblers.

One of my favorite places to look for the Arizona warblers is on Mount Ord in the Matatzal Mountains, an hour and a half northeast of Phoenix. The first or second weekend in May are ideal times to make the trip. The Matatzals are typical of many mountains ranges in central and southeastern Arizona. They rise abruptly from the desert floor to an elevation over 7,000 feet. Vegetative communities change dramatically as you climb from desert scrub at the base to pine and mixed conifer at the top. On Mount Ord, a dirt road (Forest Road 626) winds approximately seven miles to the summit. On a good day in the spring, all six warblers can be found in appropriate habitat along this route.

Chapter 3

At about mile three, near the intersection with Forest Road 1688, the road enters prime habitat for Virginia's Warbler, a belt of trees where medium-sized ponderosa pines and oaks are scattered on steep, chaparral-covered slopes. It usually doesn't take me long to hear the bird's sharp, dry "chip" note or its slurred "s-weet, s-weet" song. Virginia's Warblers can be difficult to see, however. They like to forage at about eye level in dense manzanita shrubs and live scrub oak. Their mostly gray plumage blends in well in the brush-filled habitats. Virginia's Warbler is closely related to Nashville Warbler, but is easily distinguished by the small, bright yellow patch on the upper chest and the yellow under-tail coverts. Like Nashville, it has a bold eye ring.

Virginia's Warbler was named for Mary Virginia Anderson, wife of its discoverer, US Army surgeon William Anderson. He discovered it in New Mexico in 1858. Of the six species I'm describing, Virginia's is the most widespread: it breeds in much of Nevada, Utah, Colorado, Arizona, and New Mexico, as well as parts of Wyoming, South Dakota, Idaho, Texas, and California. In Arizona, it begins arriving on breeding grounds in middle to late April. The bird nests on the ground on steep hillsides, and as summer progresses, it becomes quieter and more difficult to find. Virginia's Warblers begin leaving the state in late July. By the end of August, most have taken off for their wintering grounds in the highlands of west-central Mexico.

As I continue up the Mount Ord road, the pine trees and oaks get bigger and the chaparral changes to an understory that includes New Mexico locust and serviceberry. The area is home to one of the most beautiful of all the North American warblers, the Painted Redstart. This striking black, red, and white bird belongs to a large family of neotropical warblers called "whitestarts," so named for the white in their outer tail feathers.

No other North American warbler species is more fun to watch than the flashy Painted Redstart. It creeps along trunks and branches of oaks and pines, constantly twitching and jerking its half-opened wings, showing off its white wing patches and fanning its white-cornered tail. Painted Redstarts are bold and inquisitive birds: they respond to "pishing" or the playback of a Northern Pygmy-Owl call by approaching closely. You sometimes see pairs chasing each other across steep, brushy slopes, occasionally flying down to the ground. Best of all, they can make even a mediocre photographer look good.

Like Virginia's Warbler, the Painted Redstart is a ground-nesting species. It builds its nest on steep slopes under tree roots or clumps of grass. Its song is a rich warble, its call a distinctive whistled "sheu" that is easily learned and recognized.

The bird arrives on its Arizona breeding grounds in mid-March and stays until mid-September. A few individuals spend the winter in southeastern Arizona; during most winters, one or two can be found in Madera Canyon in the Santa Rita Mountains. The Painted Redstart is unmistakable, but keep an eye out for Slate-throated Redstart, which looks similar. It is mostly charcoal gray and has a maroon crown, and it lacks the white wing patch of the Painted. The Slate-throated species has been recorded a few times in spring in southeastern Arizona.

Grace's Warbler is found almost exclusively in pine trees, so the big pines near the summit of Mount Ord often yield sightings. The male often sings a rapid, accelerating trill while hidden behind clusters of pine needles in the very highest branches. Just when you finally spot a Grace's and get your binoculars on it, however, it always seems to fly off to the top of the next tree. Looking for this gray, white, and yellow bird can bring on an acute case of "warbler neck."

Grace's Warbler is closely related to the Yellow-throated Warbler of the East, but lacks the distinct black face and white neck spot of its counterpart. Grace's was named in honor of the sister of its discoverer, the famed 19th-century naturalist and ornithologist Elliott Coues, who first found it in pine trees in Prescott in 1864. At the time of its discovery, Coues was an army surgeon posted to the Arizona territory.

Grace's Warbler breeds from southern Nevada to western Texas and south into Mexico. Its Arizona range is almost identical to that of Virginia's Warbler. Grace's Warbler begins arriving in early to mid-April. Because it spends so much time high up in the trees, it has been notoriously difficult to study, and much of its nesting and breeding biology are still unknown. In late August, it begins to leave for its wintering grounds, which stretch from Mexico south to Nicaragua.

The Olive Warbler is the oddball of North American warblers. Studies of its behavior, physical characteristics, and DNA have shown that it's not even a warbler. It's the world's only member of the family Peucedramidae and may be more closely related to finches, tanagers, and honeycreepers than true New World warblers.

The male is both unmistakable and unforgettable. A beautiful burnt-orange head and upper breast surround his distinctive black mask. Females and young have a yellowish head and upper breast, and their masks are not as dark as the male's. It is easy to see why they are one of the most sought-after of the Arizona warblers.

I find Olive Warblers every spring on Mount Ord. These birds seem to move around constantly, often in pairs or small groups. They stay high in pines and Douglas-fir, where they creep along branches gleaning insects. Their very unwarbler-like calls and songs often announce their presence. One call in particular sounds a lot like the soft "pfew" note of a Western Bluebird. Several of their songs have a decided titmouse quality. Keep in mind that both Bridled Titmouse and Western Bluebird occur in some of the same habitat and mountain ranges as the Olive Warbler.

Female Olive Warblers can sometimes be confused with Hermit Warblers, particularly the Hermits in their first autumn of life that migrate through the mountains of Arizona in the fall. A few Olive Warblers overwinter in Arizona, sometimes descending to lower elevations. Their breeding range extends from east-central Arizona and southwestern New Mexico to Nicaragua. The northern edge of their range is near Flagstaff (and may be creeping north-ward).

The hardest of the six Arizona warblers to find on Mount Ord (but one easily found elsewhere) is the Red-faced Warbler, an-other ground-nesting species. Red-faced Warblers like cool canyon drainages and north-facing slopes with mixed conifers and Gambel oak.

If your first glimpse is from below or behind, the bird's pearly gray back and whitish underparts might suggest you are looking at a titmouse or a chickadee. Just wait until it turns and looks at you, displaying its brilliant red-and-black face. These warblers look like their head and throat were dunked in a can of bright red paint. You might have a hard time tearing yourself away from watching such beautiful birds.

The song, a series of quick "zweet" notes, sounds like a Yellow Warbler's song. The Yellow Warbler, however, is primarily a bird of valleys and lower elevations, while the Red-faced is a mountain bird found above 6,000 feet. If you're in the mountains and hear what sounds like a Yellow Warbler, think again; it might well be a Red-faced Warbler.

Though difficult to find on Mount Ord, Red-faced can be quite common in southeastern Arizona. I particularly remember a morning hike up Miller Creek in the Huachuca Mountains early one May. Red-faced Warblers seemed to be singing from every other tree.

Like Olive Warbler, Red-faced may be expanding the northern limit of its range in Arizona. We get to enjoy its presence from late April through early September, when it heads south for Mexico and Central America.

The final Arizona warbler, and one I never miss on my spring trips to Mount Ord, is Lucy's Warbler. If you stop to look for them on the way down, where the highway crosses desert washes and streams, you can usually hear them singing in the mesquite trees the minute you get out of the car. In fact, Lucy's could well be called the "Mesquite Warbler."

Lucy's is the smallest of the North American warblers. Naturalist James G. Cooper discovered it in 1861 at Fort Mohave near the Nevada border. It was named for Lucy Hunter Baird, the daughter of Smithsonian ornithologist Spencer Baird.

This tiny, pale gray warbler has a reddish-brown rump that is difficult to see. One of the most diagnostic features is the dark eye, which stands out like a button on the whitish face. By mid-August, Lucy's acquires a distinct buffy color on the breast.

Lucy's is a cavity nester. It builds its nests in natural cavities in mesquite and sycamore trees and sometimes uses abandoned woodpecker holes. The only other cavity-nesting warbler is the Prothonotary Warbler of the eastern and southeastern United States.

Lucy's Warbler arrives in March, shortly after the mesquite and sycamore trees have leafed out. It has a rapid, energetic song that sounds somewhat similar to that of the Yellow Warbler. These tiny warblers are mostly gone from the state by the end of August.

Besides Mount Ord, there are a number of other easily accessible locations in central and southeastern Arizona where you can go to look for the Arizona warblers. The Pinal Mountains, east of Phoenix near the town of Superior, are an excellent place to find them. A dirt road takes you to the top of the Pinals (7,800 feet) through all the appropriate Arizona warbler habitats. Near Tucson, all six species can be found along the Catalina Highway, which goes to the top of Mount Lemmon. They are also found throughout the mountains of southeastern Arizona, including places like Madera Canyon in the Santa Rita Mountains; Miller, Carr, and Sawmill canyons in the Huachuca Mountains; and the Chiricahua Mountains.

The Arizona warblers are easy to find in much of their breeding range. With the exception of female Olive Warblers, the sexes look similar, and their identification is straightforward and easy. In many places—particularly mountain ranges in the central and southeastern part of the state—all six can often be found in close proximity. If you need an excuse to explore Arizona's high country, the Arizona warblers make an excellent alibi.

Arizona's Woodpeckers

One morning last March, I was jarred awake by a loud, banging noise in my carport. The source of the racket was a Gila Woodpecker that had started to excavate a nest hole in an empty wall cabinet. The pounding continued for several mornings before the bird finally decided to go elsewhere, leaving behind an unfinished hole about three inches in diameter. I was relieved to have some peace and quiet, but also disappointed. I had hoped for a chance to watch the fledging of a new generation of these handsome desert woodpeckers, which are one of Arizona's 12 breeding woodpecker species.

That's right: more than half of North America's 22 woodpecker species reside in our state. These fascinating birds occupy a wide variety of habitats, ranging from desert lowlands to high-altitude spruce-fir forests. All are superbly adapted to a life of climbing and drilling in trees and cacti.

Because woodpeckers spend much of their lives pounding, drilling, and drumming on hard surfaces, they have evolved a number of physical adaptations that help them withstand constant shocks to the head. Among the adaptations are plate-like spongy head bones that cushion and distribute the force of the blows, and a small subdural space that allows for less movement of the brain inside the head during impact.

Birding Arizona

Anyone who has ever watched a woodpecker climb a tree trunk or nimbly move along the underside of a branch has probably wondered how woodpeckers climb trees without falling. The answer lies in several physical adaptations that make them uniquely suited to their arboreal lifestyle. The next time you see a woodpecker fly to a tree or saguaro cactus, notice how it sticks itself on the trunk when it lands. Woodpeckers have strong, stiff tail feathers, which they use as a prop to hold themselves against the trunks of trees or cacti. They also have strong feet. Most birds have four toes, with three facing forward and one back. Almost all woodpeckers, however, have feet with two toes facing forward and two back. This adaptation allows them to grip and cling to vertical surfaces. When climbing, they hop with both feet grasping the trunk, repositioning their tail as they move upward or sideways.

The *Picoides* and *Dryobates* Woodpeckers

American Three-toed Woodpeckers are a species I sometimes find climbing in old-growth spruce and fir trees in the forests of northern and eastern Arizona. They are black and white, with white stripes on the face and heavy barring on the sides. As their name implies, they—along with the closely related Black-backed Woodpecker—are unique in having three toes instead of four. They are the only Arizona species in the genus *Picoides,* a group that previously included four other breeding Arizona species: Hairy, Downy, Arizona, and Ladder-backed. The latter four species have recently been moved to the genus *Dryobates.*

Look for American Three-toed Woodpeckers on the San Francisco Peaks and at Sunrise Park in the White Mountains. While not particularly shy, they are unobtrusive and can be difficult to locate. One of the best ways to find them when they are not drumming is to simply stop and listen. They can sometimes be heard quietly flecking away tree bark as they search for bark beetles. Three-toed Woodpeckers make a loud and distinct drum, which is often heard in springtime. The dead and dying trees they prefer resonate with a loud, hollow "bonk, bonk" sound that tapers off at the end. Like most woodpeckers, they drum to attract mates and to announce their territories to other woodpeckers. They play an important role in maintaining healthy forests by controlling bark beetle and other insect populations. At times, they can be easy to find in recently burned forest where bark beetles are attacking dead or dying trees.

Woodpeckers use their sharp, pointed bills like chisels when foraging and excavating nest cavities. No Arizona woodpecker is better at excavating holes than the Hairy Woodpecker. It has a black-and-white-striped face, relatively long stout bill, and white back. The males show a small red patch on the nape. Hairy Woodpeckers are found at higher elevations in coniferous forests throughout much of the state and are easily located by their call, which is a loud, sharp "peek." Their abandoned nest and roost holes are often used by other cavity-nesting birds, including Flammulated Owl, Northern Pygmy-Owl, Violet-green Swallow, and Western and Mountain bluebirds. Squirrels also use these holes.

The Downy Woodpecker looks like a miniature version of the Hairy Woodpecker. In fact, one can easily be mistaken for the other. Downy, Arizona's smallest woodpecker, is found sparingly from above the Mogollon Rim north to the Kaibab Plateau and in the White Mountains. It is best distinguished from Hairy Woodpecker by its short, tiny bill, which is only about a third of the diameter of its head. Look and listen for these small woodpeckers in deciduous trees and willows along streams in the White Mountains and in aspen groves and pines on the North Rim of the Grand Canyon. Their call is a distinctive, descending "whinny."

The Arizona Woodpecker is closely related to the Hairy Woodpecker but is easily distinguished by its breast and head markings, which are a chocolate-brown color. This species is the only North American woodpecker with a solid brown back. The Arizona Woodpecker might be called "the woodpecker that can't get its name straight." Over the years, it has gone through a number of name changes, including Brown-Backed Woodpecker and Strickland's Woodpecker. Its US range lies almost entirely within Arizona, where it inhabits live oak and pine forest in Arizona's southeastern "Sky Island" mountain ranges. These handsome woodpeckers are often seen in Madera Canyon, a well-known birding area in the Santa Rita Mountains south of Tucson.

The final *Dryobates* species is the Ladder-backed Woodpecker. It is frequently encountered in low to moderate elevations in a variety of desert habitats south of the Mogollon Rim and in western Arizona. A bold, black-and-white-barred back and black-and-white striped head make it easy to identify. Males have a bright red cap. Once called the "Cactus Woodpecker," the Ladder-backed frequently excavates nest holes in palo verde trees. Its descending, whinny-like call is reminiscent of the one made by the Downy Woodpecker.

Chapter 3

The *Melanerpes* Woodpeckers

Acorn Woodpeckers look nothing like Woody Woodpecker, but they have a call that sounds like that of the famous cartoon bird. In fact, Woody's call may have been patterned after the Acorn Woodpecker's.

Along with Lewis's and Gila woodpeckers, Acorn Woodpeckers belong in the genus *Melanerpes*. They are found in pine-oak woodland in much of central and southeastern Arizona. They have a striking red, white, and black face pattern, with light-colored eyes that give them a distinctive clownish appearance. The two sexes are easy to tell apart. The male has a red cap that borders the white forehead. On the female, there is a black stripe between the red cap and the white forehead.

Often seen in small groups, Acorn Woodpeckers have a complicated cooperative breeding system, with several males often competing to mate with one female, and nonbreeding birds helping to raise the young. Much of their diet consists of insects, which they catch by flycatching from perches. They are most famous, however, for harvesting acorns, which they store in granaries—trees or utility poles with specially drilled holes into which they pound acorns to store for the winter. Trees have been known to have up to 50,000 acorn-filled holes. People who build homes and cabins in oak woodlands sometimes find these woodpeckers drilling granary holes in the eaves and wood siding of their houses.

One of the most beautiful Arizona woodpeckers is Lewis's Woodpecker. This large species is a resident of open pine forest in northern and eastern Arizona. Lewis's has a unique combination of crimson-red face, silver neck collar, glossy green back, and silvery-pink belly. It has a direct, flapping flight, unlike the undulating or roller-coaster-like flight of most woodpeckers. Like Acorn Woodpeckers, they fly out from perches to catch insects. Sometimes, they congregate in large flocks. In the fall of 2014, I observed more than 25 Lewis's Woodpeckers around the Mormon Lake Lodge south of Flagstaff. They were busy gathering and storing what appeared to be a bumper crop of acorns. In winter, Lewis's Woodpeckers sometimes disperse to lowland areas, where they can turn up in pecan groves and city parks.

The Gila Woodpecker—like the one that kept waking me up last March—is one of the iconic birds of the Sonoran Desert. Its US range is almost entirely in Arizona, where it is a permanent resident of desert scrub and riparian woodland in much of the central and southern parts of the state. It has a tan head and underparts, and black-and-white barring on the back, wings, and tail. The male shows a small red patch on his crown. These handsome birds are very noisy, often giving raucous calls that sound like "geet geet geet." They are often found in urban areas, especially where there are saguaro cacti. In flight, they show white wing patches, which gives birders an easy way to tell them apart from Ladder-backed Woodpeckers, which occupy much of the same habitat. Gila Woodpeckers are famous for excavating nest holes in saguaros. Their abandoned holes are used by other species, including Western Screech-Owl, Elf Owl, American Kestrel, Ash-throated and Brown-crested flycatchers, and European Starling.

Chapter 3

The *Colaptes* Woodpeckers

When I was young, I loved to watch Northern Flickers in autumn, feeding on the purple berries of the Virginia creeper that grew on the side of our neighbor's house in Flagstaff. These colorful woodpeckers are members of the genus *Colaptes.* Arizona has two breeding flicker species. The Northern Flicker nests in the forests of northern and eastern Arizona and migrates to lowland areas in winter. The Gilded Flicker is a permanent resident of the Sonoran Desert.

Flickers have a distinctive black bib patch, spotted breast, and long stout bill. In flight, they show a conspicuous white rump and colorful wing linings, which are reddish in the Northern and yellowish in the Gilded. These opportunistic feeders are often seen hopping about on the ground, snaring ants with their long, sticky tongues. They even visit hummingbird feeders, hanging precariously as they sip sugar water. Flickers have a loud drum and a call that sounds like "clear." Gilded Flickers, like Gila Woodpeckers, show a preference for excavating nest holes in saguaros.

The *Sphyrapicus* Woodpeckers

Two sapsuckers, Williamson's and Red-naped, both in the genus *Sphyrapicus*, round out Arizona's 12 breeding woodpecker species. The striking male Williamson's Sapsucker is mostly black with a yellow belly, red throat, and large white wing patch. The female is much plainer, with a barred back and brownish head. These rather shy woodpeckers are often found in aspen groves in coniferous forests in northern and eastern Arizona. The Red-naped

Sapsucker has a black-and-white-striped face and red crown, with red on the nape. It occupies the same range and habitats as Williamson's. In winter, both species migrate into lowland areas.

Sapsuckers get their name from the neat rows of sap wells they drill into trees. Once these are drilled, they frequently return to them, feeding on the oozing sap. Sapsucker wells not only feed the woodpecker itself but other bird species, including Broad-tailed and Black-chinned hummingbirds.

Rare Woodpeckers

Arizona is also visited on occasion by several rare transient woodpecker species that show up mostly in fall and winter. Among them are Red-breasted and Yellow-bellied sapsuckers and Red-headed Woodpecker (accidental). In addition, there are a number of records of Yellow-shafted Flicker, a subspecies of the Northern Flicker.

Many species, including humans, benefit either directly or indirectly from the activities of woodpeckers. These birds play an important role in the natural world by controlling insect populations and providing homes for many other birds and mammals. Sometimes, woodpeckers can be a nuisance and create conflicts with their pounding and drumming. These inconveniences, however, are greatly outweighed by the good they do. You can find woodpeckers just about anywhere you travel in Arizona. The next time you see one, stop to observe it. Whether climbing up a tree, drumming on a rooftop, or noisily chasing usurpers away from its nest cavity, a woodpecker is always fun to watch.

Chapter 3

Two Fascinating Arizona Corvids

In the distance, I could see dozens of birds in the trees. Occasionally, white patches flashed from tails and wings as the birds hopped from branch to branch or flew down to the ground. I drew closer and soon realized I was watching two quintessentially western Corvid species, the Clark's Nutcracker and the Pinyon Jay.

Individual birds were hammering at pine cones held fast with their feet. They were Clark's Nutcrackers, busy at work in cone-laden pinyon pine trees growing along the sides of a small canyon. Higher up, along the rim, scores of Pinyon Jays were moving through the trees and walking about on the boulder-strewn slope, each one probing the ground with its black bill.

Large flocks of Pinyon Jays are a fairly common sight along the South Fork of the Little Colorado River in eastern Arizona. Large numbers of Clark's Nutcrackers, however, are another matter. They're usually seen in mixed conifer or spruce-fir habitat at much higher elevations. Most often, it is a single bird giving its raspy, grating call while perched atop a limber pine, or a small group flying at treetop level through the forest.

Watching on that September morning, I was struck not only by the sheer number of birds, but (because I was seeing both species together) by how alike they look in silhouette or profile. In fact, they share many physical and behavioral traits that make them uniquely suited to what they were doing that morning—collecting, transporting, and caching pine seeds.

Many people's first encounter with Clark's Nutcracker is at a scenic viewpoint or campground in a western national park, where it is often seen hopping about in search of food handouts. Its range extends from central British Columbia and western Alberta south through Washington, Oregon, and much of the Intermountain West to Arizona and New Mexico. This strikingly handsome bird sports a whitish-gray head and underparts set off by jet-black wings. It has a long, sharply pointed bill, and its short tail and long wings show white patches in flight, making it easy to spot as it flies through the trees.

Clark's Nutcracker is named for Captain William Clark of Lewis and Clark fame, who first observed and described it in Idaho during the expedition in 1805. Perhaps, while watching the bird pecking and hacking away at a pine cone, Clark mistakenly thought it was a new species of woodpecker, an error that was later caught by expedition leader Meriwether Lewis, who correctly put it in the family Corvidae, which includes the jays and crows.

Pinyon Jay occurs over a large portion of the interior western United States. It ranges from central Oregon east to western South Dakota and south to Baja California and central New Mexico. Go looking for it, however, and it seems to be one of those birds you see either dozens of or none at all. This is in part due to the fact that the species is very social. Birds nest in colonies, building a single bulky, well-insulated nest per tree, and live in large, roving communal flocks that at times can number in the hundreds. There are, however, exceptions to this all-or-nothing rule. I remember once trying to find a Pinyon Jay for a visitor from Minnesota who badly wanted it for a life bird. After searching all afternoon without success, we spotted a bird sitting atop a tree in the distance. It turned out to be a lone Pinyon Jay, and yes, it was perched on a pinyon pine tree.

Chapter 3

Unlike its flashy nutcracker cousin, the Pinyon Jay is a rather dull, uniform blue color. Like the nutcracker, it has a prominent sharp-pointed bill. The jay's generic name *Gymnorhinus* (composed of *gymnos*, the Greek word for "naked," and *rhinos*, the Greek word for "nose") refers to the fact that the base of the bill is featherless, an adaptation that allows the bird to probe deep into pitch-laden pine cones. The Pinyon Jay's call is a loud quavering "queh, queh" that carries long distances and seems to echo through the trees. Perhaps no other bird call is more strongly associated with western pinyon-juniper woodland.

Both Pinyon Jays and Clark's Nutcrackers are omnivores. They eat a wide range of foods but prefer pine seeds when available. In winter, however, they are almost entirely dependent on seeds they collected and cached the previous autumn. Indeed, both species begin nesting in late winter or early spring, earlier than just about any other North American songbird. They are able to do this because of the energy provided by the hidden seeds; they don't have to wait for other food to become available in spring. Other birds—notably woodpeckers, nuthatches, and chickadees—also set food aside for later, but not nearly to the same extent. Individual Clark's Nutcrackers and Pinyon Jays will cache tens of thousands of seeds in thousands of different cache sites in years when seed crops are good.

They do it by thrusting their bill into the ground, depositing a few seeds, and then covering their cache with dirt, pebbles, or even leaf litter. Pinyon Jays primarily cache seeds of the pinyon pine, while Clark's Nutcrackers set aside the seeds of mostly higher-elevation pine trees. On occasion, large numbers of Clark's Nutcrackers will move into the lower-elevation pinyon pine forest in search of seeds, as I observed them doing along the South Fork of the Little Colorado River that crisp autumn day.

The relationship between Pinyon Jay, Clark's Nutcracker, and pine trees is often described as "codependent," and it may actually be driving the evolution of both the trees and the birds. The relationship is mutually beneficial: each has become dependent on the other. In exchange for a reliable source of nutritious food, the jays and nutcrackers perpetuate the pine forest by dispersing and planting the tree's "wingless" seeds. From forgotten or overlooked seed caches, saplings grow. Consequently, both birds play an important role in replanting treeless areas in the West.

In the first edition of his field guide, David Sibley placed Pinyon Jay and Clark's Nutcracker together under the heading of "specialized jays." Ornithologist Russell Balda, emeritus Regents' Professor (retired) at Northern Arizona University, is one of the leading authorities on these two species. He believes that Pinyon Jay may be evolving away or "diverging" from relatives like the Mexican Jay and Scrub Jay, and converging on the Nutcracker. As he puts it: "The Pinyon Jay appears to be a Nutcracker 'want-to-be.'"

Pinyon Jays and Clark's Nutcrackers have evolved a number of physical characteristics that make them superbly adapted to life in the pines. Both have long wings and are powerful fliers. Clark's Nutcracker, in particular, is known to make repeated long-distance, high-altitude flights from seed-collecting sites to caching areas that can be up to about 13 miles away.

Birds of both species use their long, sharply pointed bill to probe the ground when caching and collecting seeds. They also use it to determine the thickness of the seed coat, test whether a seed is empty or full, and most importantly, hack open and shred un-opened pine cones. Pinyon Jay and Clark's Nutcracker, unlike other western jay species, do not have to wait for cones to open naturally to extract seeds. When you compare the size and shape of the bills of these two species with those of Woodhouse's Scrub Jay and Mexican Jay, two species that are much less reliant on seed caches, it is easy to see why: the bills of Pinyon Jay and Clark's Nutcracker are sturdier and sharper.

Other interesting and unique adaptations allow Pinyon Jays and Clark's Nutcrackers to hold and transport large numbers of seeds. The nutcracker drops pine seeds through an opening at the base of its tongue into a special pouch (called a "sublingual pouch") that is nothing short of amazing. An elastic, saclike extension of the floor of the mouth, it can swell enough to hold up to 95 seeds, which represents almost 13 percent of the bird's total body weight. Pinyon Jay has evolved a similar adaptation—an expandable esophagus that allows it to hold and carry pinyon pine seeds. When full, the esophagus can hold up to 40 seeds, representing about 12 percent of the bird's total body weight.

It is one thing to collect and cache seeds and quite another to be able to return later and find them, yet both of these species do this with astonishing accuracy. Clark's Nutcrackers have been observed flying directly to cache sites and digging through deep snow or even pecking through ice to retrieve seeds they'd hidden 8 to 10 months earlier. Scientists estimate that a Clark's will relocate up to two-thirds of the seeds it cached up to 13 months later. How does it refind seeds in altered landscapes many months after hiding them?

To find out, Balda and colleague Alan C. Kamil of the

University of Nebraska–Lincoln studied the two species extensively in northern Arizona, where they occur together around the San Francisco Peaks, and also conducted laboratory experiments on the birds' ability to recover caches. The researchers hypothesized that the more a species depends on cached food for its survival in winter when no other food is available, the better its spatial memory would be, and the results proved them to be correct.

Both Pinyon Jay and Clark's Nutcracker demonstrated exceptional ability to find hidden seeds, and they were significantly better at it than the closely related Woodhouse's Scrub Jay and Mexican Jay, which inhabit lower, warmer woodlands and are less dependent on caches for survival. These laboratory experiments suggested that Pinyon Jay and Clark's Nutcracker use both landmarks and internal compasses to navigate almost unerringly to cache sites.

When cone crops fail, both Pinyon Jay and Clark's Nutcracker are known to wander. Pinyon Jay may irrupt in all directions: west to central and southeastern California; north to northern Idaho and western Montana; east to Nebraska and western Kansas; and south to western Texas, northern Sonora, and northern Chihuahua. Irruptions of Clark's Nutcracker may carry birds to the California coast and as far east as western Ontario in Canada and Pennsylvania, Illinois, and Arkansas in the United States.

I can't help but smile every time I see these two remarkable species. The next time you're out looking for them, take time to watch and observe them carefully as they fly off with pilfered food from a campground, hack away at a pine cone, or cache seeds alongside scores of their kin. Their behavior speaks volumes about their biology, habitat preference, and breeding habitats, and even their evolution.

The Arizona Wrens

When you think wrens, think beautiful songs and distinctive call notes. North America is home to 10 different wren species, all of which have occurred in Arizona. Seven of these (Cactus, Canyon, Rock, Bewick's, Marsh, House, and Pacific) breed in Arizona, while three others (Carolina, Winter, and Sedge) occur in the state on occasion as vagrants. Another species, the Sinaloa Wren, was first found in the state in 2008, and there have now been several additional records of this Mexican species. The wrens, perhaps more than any other bird group, illustrate the importance of learning and memorizing birdsongs.

The wrens are a group of small, active birds, mostly brownish in color, with sharp, pointed bills. They are often seen foraging in dense vegetation, searching and probing for insects in crevices, under leaves, and behind tree bark. Probably more than any other group, they fit the name "little brown jobs" or "LBJs," a term often given by non-birders to small, nondescript birds.

While mostly unremarkable in their plumage characteristics, the wrens have beautiful songs, and several are considered among North America's finest songsters. Their songs and call notes often help birders find and identify these birds, which are sometimes hard to see as they skulk or quickly fly away. In Arizona, it is not at all uncommon, especially during the winter months, for birders to tally as many as five or six different wren species in a single day.

The Cactus Wren is North America's largest and Arizona's best-known wren. In fact it's the Arizona state bird. Cactus Wrens have a large, whitish eyestripe that extends well back onto the head, with a heavily spotted breast and buffy brown underparts. It is probably the least musical of the wrens, with a raspy song that is often described as the sound of a car engine turning over. Cactus Wrens are famous for building their nests in the middle of cholla cactus, a strategy that affords their nests protection from predators. Their range is restricted to the central, southern, and western parts of the state, where they commonly inhabit arid desert scrub habitat. These wrens can also be found in urban areas, especially where people plant cholla and other cactus.

If the Cactus Wren has the least musical song, the Canyon Wren has, by most accounts, the most beautiful song of the Arizona wrens. A series of descending liquid notes spirals down the scale and seems to echo and bounce off canyon walls and cliffs. The Canyon Wren inhabits rocky outcroppings, canyons, and cliffs, and is found in suitable habitat in most parts of the state. Unlike the Cactus Wren, it is seldom found in urban settings.

While taking nothing away from the Cactus Wren, I have always believed that if any wren was going to be selected as the Arizona state bird, it should have been the Canyon Wren. First of all, the Canyon Wren has a much wider distribution in the state. It is also commonly found in canyons—and after all, this is the Grand Canyon State! The colors of the Canyon Wren—bright rufous contrasting with a white throat—are a real standout. But above all else, the Canyon Wren's voice is virtually without peer among the wrens, or most other birds for that matter. That's why it has my vote for state bird.

The Rock Wren is the state's second-largest wren species. It's a bird I seem to stumble into unexpectedly in a variety of habitats; on rocky desert hillsides broiling under the Arizona sun, or above timberline in alpine habitat at the top of the San Francisco Peaks, where it often gives its characteristic "tick-ear" call from rocky talus slopes. The song of the Rock Wren is a variable series of phrases, often repeated three or more times. The repetition and variation remind me somewhat of a Northern Mockingbird.

Rock Wrens build a very curious entranceway to their nests. I once watched one disappear into a crevice on the side of Camelback Mountain in Phoenix. Investigating the crevice, I noticed that the entranceway leading into the nest was paved with small, flattish stones. Why Rock Wrens go to the trouble to construct these rocky pathways is unknown.

Another of the larger breeding Arizona wren species is Bewick's. This wren is widely distributed around the state. It is often found in riparian habitats, but especially in pinyon-juniper woodland. The southwestern population is noticeably grayer in color than the population in the eastern United States, which is decidedly browner on the back and head. Bewick's Wren has a very long tail and a distinct long, white eyeline.

This wren's song is highly variable, with pronounced differences between eastern, southwestern, and Pacific populations. The typical song it makes in Arizona is a slurred introductory note followed by a trill that is sometimes described as the dial return of an old rotary phone. Even within Arizona, however, there are noticeable differences. The *Arizona Breeding Bird Atlas* notes that Bewick's Wrens in the northern third of the state sing a song that sounds much like that of a Song Sparrow. One time at Ganado Lake, I heard what I thought was a singing Song Sparrow hopping about on the lower limbs of a large cottonwood tree. Sure enough, it turned out to be a Bewick's Wren. My rule of thumb for birding in Arizona: If you hear a voice you don't recognize, first try to rule out Bewick's Wren.

Besides their elaborate and musical songs, wrens have a variety of calls. These vocalizations are well worth taking the time to learn. Although many of these calls are distinctive, they can sometimes be confused with the calls of other species. For example, in winter, House Wrens are frequently found in dense, brushy vegetation in lowland desert areas of Arizona. They give a scolding call that, to my ears, sounds much like that of a Black-tailed Gnatcatcher, which commonly occurs in the same habitat. The House Wren also gives a classic and distinctive "comb call," which sounds like someone running a finger along the teeth of a hair comb. The Canyon Wren often gives a "jzeet" call at the end of its song. When given in isolation and heard at a distance, this call can remind you of one of the varied calls of the Rock Wren. As we shall see, the call notes of the Pacific and Winter wrens—which both occur in Arizona—are one of the more reliable ways of separating these two difficult species.

At the end of a long, hot, southern Arizona summer, you always know cooler temperatures are not far off and relief is near at hand when you're out birding and hear a returning Marsh Wren giving its exuberant, raspy song from deep in cattails or bulrushes. These handsome wrens breed very locally in Arizona, mostly along the lower Colorado River. Most are migratory winter residents that can be quite common in their preferred wetland habitat. When you manage to get a look at one climbing up or hanging onto a cattail, they're quite beautiful. Marsh Wrens have a pale breast with a reddish back and scapulars and, like many other wren species, have a distinct white eyestripe. One of the instant identifying features of these medium-sized wrens is the white stripes on the bird's upper back.

The House Wren is one of the smaller of the breeding Arizona wren species. In summertime, they're often seen at relatively high elevations along forest edges and in mountain drainages. During the winter months, they move into lowland areas of the state, where they are sometimes encountered in dense, brushy areas in riparian or desert habitat. It seems you almost always hear their raspy calls before you manage to get a look.

The House Wren has a plain face, with just a hint of an eyestripe. The plain face is a good field mark for separating this species from a number of other Arizona wrens, which have bold and distinct eyestripes. House Wrens have a fairly short tail, which they often hold up in a cocked position. Their beautiful song is composed of lively trills and buzzes.

A race or subspecies of the House Wren, the Brown-throated Wren, occurs in the mountains of southeastern Arizona in ranges like the Huachucas and Santa Ritas. At one time, it was actually considered a separate species. It is a much browner bird with a distinct, warm buffy-brown throat.

The smallest Arizona wren is the Pacific Wren. These sprites average about 4 inches in length. Perhaps their most diagnostic feature is a very short tail, which they frequently hold up in a cocked position.

Pacific Wrens have a beautiful song, which seems to bubble along incessantly as they skulk and hide in piles of wood and brush. The high-pitched series of buzzes, tinkles, and trills seems to test the limits of human hearing. I've heard this song, or at least parts of it, in late fall and late winter while walking along the upper reaches of Oak Creek Canyon and the West Fork of Oak Creek.

Pacific Wren has the most limited breeding area of any of the Arizona wrens, with the only confirmed breeding taking place along the Mogollon Rim above Payson. It may also breed in the Oak Creek/West Fork area. There is a considerable influx of non-breeding Pacific Wrens into Arizona in winter.

In 2010, the American Ornithologists' Union split the Pacific Wren from its eastern counterpart, the Winter Wren. There have now been a few confirmed sightings and accepted records of Winter Wren in Arizona. Trying to differentiate these two species visually in the field can be a real challenge.

The Winter Wren is said to have a more whitish throat as compared to the darker-brown throat of the Pacific Wren. The Winter Wren also tends to have more spotting on the back and wing coverts, but these plumage differences are subtle and difficult to see in the field. Most Arizona birders attempt to separate the two on the basis of their call notes. The notes of the Pacific Wren are often compared to the chip notes of a Wilson's Warbler, while that of the Winter Wren is akin to the call note of a Song Sparrow.

The status of the Pacific and Winter wrens in Arizona during the winter months remains unclear, in large part because of identification difficulties and the considerable fluctuation in numbers of nonbreeding Pacific Wrens from year to year. Pacific Wren, however, remains the more likely species to see in Arizona during winter. Look for both species in riparian areas in central and southeastern Arizona. They particularly seem to like areas where piles of flood debris and exposed tree roots provide cover.

Besides the Winter Wren, two other eastern wrens have occurred in Arizona as rare vagrants: the Carolina and the Sedge. In 1999, a birder familiar with the song of the Carolina Wren heard one singing at Cook's Lake, on the San Pedro River. Along with several other birders, I went to search for it. We spent several hours trying to see it, but only got brief glimpses as the bird continuously moved around through the tops of tall cottonwood and mesquite trees. Although we never got a good look, we did hear its beautiful song, which it sang occasionally from perches high in the trees. There are still just a handful of Arizona records of Carolina Wren, and only recently has Arizona recorded its first confirmed Sedge Wren, which appeared in November 2010 at Peña Blanca Lake.

The first Sinaloa Wren to be documented in the United States was found in southeastern Arizona in August 2008. The arrival of this Mexican species had been predicted due to its range, which extends well up into Sonora. In fact, there were reports of its ranging as close as 60 miles from the border. Two experienced birders were birding at The Nature Conservancy's Patagonia-Sonoita Creek Preserve when one of them heard an unfamiliar song from up in a cottonwood tree. They knew immediately the song was out of place. The other birder, who was familiar with the song from a visit to Mexico, soon realized they were listening to a Sinaloa Wren. In 2012, another Sinaloa Wren was found along the Santa Cruz

River by an experienced birder who recognized its voice coming from thick vegetation along the river.

These remarkable finds underscore the importance of learning and memorizing birdsongs. Southern Arizona birders might be well advised to learn the songs of a number of Mexican species that, like the Sinaloa Wren, have been predicted to find their way to Arizona.

Watching Hawks

The Santa Cruz River

They were little more than dots in the sky, circling and drifting north on the late-morning thermals. Broad wings and a short, stubby tail gave us the initial impression they were Black Vultures, which are fairly common in south-central Arizona. Suddenly, as one of them banked to the left, we saw a white tail band flashing in the sunlight. No, they were not Black Vultures. They were the birds that I—along with several other birders—had come to watch: Common Black-Hawks.

That morning we were at what has become an increasingly popular hawk-watching site along the Santa Cruz River near Tubac, Arizona. Tubac is about 50 miles south of Tucson and about 160 miles southeast of Phoenix. Every March, birders gather here to witness the annual spring migration of Common Black-Hawks. Tubac is the only place in the United States where these large neotropical raptors can be reliably seen in migration, and often in good numbers.

In early March, Common Black-Hawks begin migrating up

the Santa Cruz River, which flows north from Mexico into Arizona, eventually joining the Gila River. Their numbers usually build to a peak sometime between March 10 and March 25. On any given day during this period, it's not unusual to see up to 10 migrating Common Black-Hawks. Actual numbers can vary depending on weather conditions. Most days, the hawks—some of which have roosted overnight—begin flying over by midmorning, getting lift from the sun-heated air. Exceptional daily tallies from along the Santa Cruz River during this time have been nothing short of amazing, with reports of 40 and even 60 birds.

Along most of its course, the Santa Cruz River is a dry riverbed, but a 15-mile stretch between Nogales and Tubac has a permanent flow of water. This area boasts a lush riparian forest dominated by mature cottonwood and willow, with scattered mesquite bosques on the river's flanks in the outer floodplain. In early March, cottonwoods and willows leaf out, and the landscape transforms into a bright green corridor winding through the Sonoran Desert.

This ribbon of vegetation attracts riparian-specialist Common Black-Hawks as they migrate from wintering grounds in Mexico to disperse and nest along rivers and creeks across central Arizona. Although no figures are available, a significant percentage of Arizona's nesting Common Black-Hawk population undoubtedly migrates along the Santa Cruz river corridor in the spring.

Most of the Common Black-Hawk's US breeding range is in Arizona, although small numbers also occur in southwestern New Mexico, western Texas, southern Utah, and southern Nevada. South of the United States, Common Black-Hawks breed throughout much of middle America, on some islands in the Caribbean

Sea, and south to northern South America. Throughout their range, Common Black-Hawks prefer areas with permanent water flows. In the United States, they often build their nests in deciduous trees like sycamores and cottonwoods. If an observer approaches a nest site too closely, the adults become agitated and warn the intruder with a series of short, whistled notes.

These hawks primarily eat aquatic reptiles and amphibians: adults hunt from streamside perches. They have also developed a taste for crayfish, a destructive exotic species now found in many Arizona rivers and streams.

At Tubac, birders watch the Common Black-Hawk migration at Ron Morris Park and from openings in the forest canopy along the Anza Trail. Those who come to watch this yearly spectacle are seldom disappointed. Common Black-Hawks are seen in a variety of situations, sometimes circling high overhead in groups or "kettles" of a dozen or more, sometimes soaring directly overhead, and sometimes even flapping at eye level through the trees. In flight, the distinctive body shape and wide white tail band are their most prominent field marks.

If you're lucky, you might see one of these beautiful hawks perched close by on a tree branch. Common Black-Hawks are extensively sooty black, with long yellow legs and a bright yellow "cere" (the area of bare skin around the beak). On perched birds, the tail appears short, and the white tail band is often visible. When observed close up, the dark plumage often shows a brownish tinge, making it appear as if the hawk has just flown through a dust storm.

Common Black-Hawks are not the only birds of prey that

migrate along the Santa Cruz river corridor in springtime. Another large neotropical raptor, the Zone-tailed Hawk, is regularly spotted, although in substantially fewer numbers than the Black-Hawk. If high-flying Common Black-Hawks can sometimes be confused with Black Vultures, Zone-tailed Hawks can easily be confused with another common vulture species, the Turkey Vulture. The Zone-tailed's underwing pattern and flight style closely mimic the Turkey Vulture's. Indeed, it is easy to overlook a Zone-tailed Hawk in a circling group of Turkey Vultures. When it is clearly visible, however, the Zone-tailed's black-and-white-banded tail usually reveals its true identity.

Hawk watchers at Tubac often see and hear yet another neotropical raptor, the Gray Hawk. These elegant hawks nest in the area and usually arrive as the Common Black-Hawks are passing through. Gray Hawks are often detected by their call—a loud, plaintive whistle. They're sometimes spotted flying through the mesquite bosques or even perched on telephone poles along the highway frontage road between Tubac and the Tumacácori National Historical Park. To add to the hawk-watching fun, a number of other hawk species are regularly seen along the riparian corridor; among them, Red-tailed, Swainson's, Sharp-shinned, and Cooper's. On rare occasions, you might even catch sight of a Crested Caracara.

The Santa Cruz river ecosystem supports many bird species. In fact, this riparian area has the highest diversity of bird species of any habitat in the country, with over 180 species being recorded. Birders walking along the Anza Trail at Tubac can enjoy many nesting species, including Vermilion Flycatcher, Blue Grosbeak, Yellow-breasted Chat, Lazuli Bunting, Broad-billed Hummingbird, Summer Tanager, Hooded Oriole, and Northern Cardinal, to name just a few. The area is also home to several species that are highly sought after by out-of-state birders. Rufous-winged Sparrow nests in the mesquite trees along the river's edge. On occasion, the Northern Beardless-Tyrannulet can be heard giving its beautiful, descending song. And both Varied Bunting and Tropical Kingbird reach the near northern limit of their breeding range in the area, arriving later in the spring.

The Grand Canyon

Exactly six months later and about 350 miles north of Tubac, we were standing on the edge of the South Rim of the Grand Canyon, watching a different hawk migration. This time, it was fall raptor migration, and the birds were flying south.

Every autumn, thousands of raptors (hawks, falcons, and vultures) cross the Grand Canyon on their annual southward migration. Since 1997, HawkWatch International observers and birders have gathered on the canyon's South Rim to watch and record this amazing passage. On average, 7,000 to 10,000 migrating raptors are recorded at Yaki and nearby Lipan points during fall migration, with 19 different species being observed at least once.

The Grand Canyon's thermal-creating topography and wide-open vistas make it ideal for hawk watching. My favorite place to observe hawks is at Yaki Point, a short distance from the canyon's main visitor center. Here, the raptors cross the canyon and fly up and over the South Rim through a large recess formed by the intersecting walls of Yaki and Mather points.

On average, about 65 migrating raptors a day are counted at Yaki Point. However, this number can vary greatly from day to day.

Chapter 3

On one late September visit, we counted 50 migrating raptors. The day before, observers counted an amazing 390. Much of this variation depends on the weather. On that particular visit, a cold front with strong winds and rains had passed through earlier in the week. It probably created a bottleneck of raptors waiting to cross in calm weather, which they did in very large numbers the day before we arrived.

As you look out from Yaki Point, views of the canyon are spectacular. On the horizon, you can make out the purple outline of Mount Trumbull on the distant Uinkaret Plateau. Among the canyon's many rock formations and talus slopes, you can pick out two prominent rock monuments: the Shiva and Isis temples. They seem to change color and shape throughout the day as sunlight and shadows play off the rocks. At Yaki Point, birders can also look down into the canyon and see small segments of the South Kaibab Trail far below. If you are lucky, you might see one of the canyon's famous mule trains carrying supplies to Phantom Ranch at the bottom of the canyon.

Early in the morning, many of the day's migrating raptors are seen in the distance over Mather Point to the northwest. One morning, I watched two Common Ravens dive-bombing and harassing a migrating Osprey. Even at a distance, you could make out the Osprey's distinctive black-and-white face pattern and diagnostic crooked wings.

As the day progresses, the air heats up, and raptors begin to appear straight out from the observation site, soaring on rising thermals. On a good day, there can be as many as a dozen raptors in view. On occasion, they will fly directly overhead. Most spectac-

111

ularly, however, they are often spotted under the rim of the canyon, hundreds of feet directly below you. In fact, in the afternoons, this is where many migrating raptors are first observed. They slowly begin winding and spiraling up toward the rim. As they circle, they appear against the cliffs and rock formations of Mather Point, climbing up through a rock record of the earth's history. As they soar and flap, they are framed against dark red cliffs of Redwall Limestone, then against the smaller cliffs and talus slopes of the Supai Group, then the whitish walls of Coconino Sandstone, and finally the sheer face of Kaibab Limestone. HawkWatch observers often use these rock formations as reference points to help each other spot and follow flying raptors.

It's always a thrill to look down at flying raptors from above. One of the less commonly seen raptors is a migrating Ferruginous Hawk. This large hawk looks spectacular from above, with a pinkish-white tail and long, narrow wings that show distinct white window panels. From above, a migrating Swainson's Hawk appears mostly dark, unlike the usual view from underneath that shows bold underwing and breast markings. Swainson's Hawks are on a long fall journey that will take them to wintering grounds in northern Argentina.

On occasion, a resident juvenile Turkey Vulture will begin drifting out of the canyon. The juveniles are easily distinguished from adults by their blackish heads. Seen from above, the back of these young birds is quite beautiful, with crisp brown feathering that shows an iridescent blue-green cast.

American Kestrels are often underappreciated by birders because they are so common. However, to watch a soaring male kestrel, its reddish back and bluish wings framed against a towering white cliff, gives one a new appreciation for the beauty and agility of these small falcons.

Along with Red-tailed Hawks and American Kestrels, two accipiters, the Cooper's and Sharp-shinned hawks, are the raptors most frequently observed during fall migration. Yaki Point provides birders an opportunity to study and compare these two look-alike members of the genus *Accipiter*. There's an old saying about trying to tell Cooper's and Sharp-shinned hawks apart when they are flying: "There are those who can't, and those who only think they can." Actually, most of these can be safely identified with a little practice. Looking down on the two species from above, they appear remarkably similar: solid bluish-gray, with darkish bands across the tail. As they circle and climb up to the rim, however, you begin to spot subtle differences: the larger head, longer head projection, and more rounded, white-tipped tail of Cooper's, versus the shorter head projection, curved leading wing edge, and square tail of Sharp-shinned. Of course, there are always a few that even the most experienced hawk watchers must write down simply as "*Accipiter* (sp)." At Yaki Point, it seems you never run out of accipiters to watch.

The star of the fall raptor migration is the Broad-winged Hawk. These small woodland buteos are casual migrants in Arizona, with only infrequent and scattered sightings, mostly in springtime. At the South Rim, however, they can be seen reliably every fall, although in very small numbers. Broad-winged Hawks are famous for their spectacular migrations down the East Coast of the United States through Mexico to their wintering grounds in South America. Along this route, they often fly in kettles, some including thousands of birds.

At the Grand Canyon, Broad-winged Hawks are usually observed from mid-September through early October as single migrants. There is a well-defined peak passage between September 23 and September 30. Most are light-morph adults, easily distinguished by their wide black-and-white tail bands and broad wings with dark borders. Many Arizona birders see their life or state Broad-winged Hawk here.

If you need a break from watching raptors and want to look at other birds, you need only turn away from the rim and explore the surrounding forest. Yaki Point, like much of the South Rim, is situated in pinyon-juniper habitat with scattered ponderosa pine and Gambel oak. In late September, cliffrose is in bloom. A large bush with fragrant white flowers, it is frequently browsed by mule deer, which are common in the national park. In this pinyon-juniper woodland, you can usually hear and spot Pinyon Jays and, less commonly, Clark's Nutcrackers. Both of these remarkable corvids spend much of their time in autumn searching for pinyon pine seeds, which they collect, transport, and cache for the upcoming winter. Other species frequently seen in the area include Woodhouse's Scrub Jay, Juniper Titmouse, White-breasted Nuthatch, and Violet-green Swallow.

Yaki Point is one of the best places in the United States to see a very special resident raptor, the California Condor. These endangered birds were reintroduced into the Grand Canyon area in 1996. At present, there are about 80 free-flying Condors in Arizona. They can be seen from Yaki Point and other locations along the South Rim almost daily from March through October. When you see one soaring in the distance, you might think you are looking at an airplane. California Condors are massive, with a wingspans over nine feet—the largest of any North American bird. At Yaki Point, they often fly in quite close, sometimes right overhead, giving hawk watchers thrilling views.

Yaki Point is one of the premier raptor-watching spots in the United States. Imagine the incomparable views you get of the Grand Canyon as you gaze out toward the North Rim on a clear September afternoon. Then, imagine half a dozen migrating raptors floating on rising thermals framed against the canyon's rock formations and cliffs. It's a sight you will likely never forget.

Birding Arizona

Special Topic:
When to Look for Rare and Unusual Species

Did you ever wonder which months of the year are best for going out and finding rare bird species in Arizona?

A friend, Professor Michael Moore, did an analysis based upon 1,651 reported rarities in the Arizona Field Ornithologists photo archive. Based on his analysis, the top four months of the year are November, January, May, and December. Slower months for rarities are June and July, with the slowest being March.

Moore breaks down the percentages by month in the following chart:

Month	# of Rarities	%
January	203	12 %
February	116	7 %
March	71	4 %
April	93	6 %
May	190	12 %
June	96	6 %
July	76	5 %
August	118	7 %
September	137	8 %
October	131	8 %
November	236	14 %
December	184	11 %
	Total 1,651	100 %

Chapter 4: Places to Go

Arizona has a number of famous birding locations. They include places like Madera Canyon, the Chiricahua Mountains, the Patagonia-Sonoita Creek Preserve, and Miller Canyon. These places are well known and have been written about extensively in bird guidebooks. Rather than re-cover that ground, I'm going to introduce you to some lesser-known but equally exciting birding locations, a number of which are in northern Arizona, where I grew up. Before we head north, though, we'll start out in "Birding the Phoenix Metropolitan Area" learning about some great places to bird in and around Phoenix. Then we will go "Birding the San Francisco Peaks," jump over the Grand Canyon to the North Rim to go "Birding the Kaibab Plateau," swing out through the vast tribal lands of the Navajo and Hopi in "Chasing Rarities Across Northeastern Arizona," and end up along the US–Mexico border, "Visiting the San Rafael Valley Grasslands." Wherever you find yourself in Arizona, whether as a resident or visitor, this chapter has a new place you'll enjoy exploring.

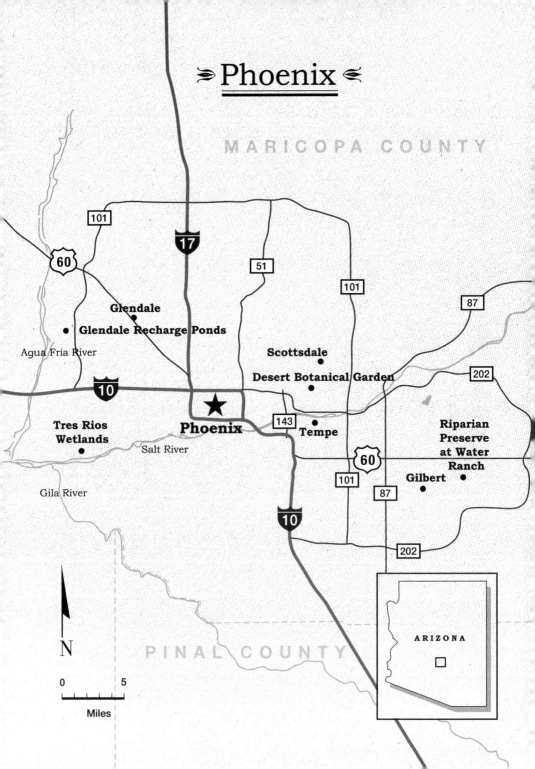

≈ Phoenix ≈

MARICOPA COUNTY

101

17

60

51

101

87

Glendale

Glendale Recharge Ponds

Agua Fria River

Scottsdale

Desert Botanical Garden

202

10

143

101

87

Tres Rios Wetlands

Phoenix

Salt River

Tempe

Riparian Preserve at Water Ranch

Gilbert

60

Gila River

101

87

10

202

N

0   5

Miles

ARIZONA

PINAL COUNTY

Chapter 4

Birding the Phoenix Metropolitan Area

Metropolitan Phoenix offers resident and visiting birders many excellent birding opportunities. Besides a number of well-known and popular birding locations—some of which will be discussed in this section—birders can find good places to bird right in their own neighborhood or at one the area's numerous parks and preserves.

Over the last hundred years as the Phoenix area has grown, so has the number of artificial lakes and ponds. Today, we live in a desert environment surrounded by water bodies large and small that have been built in subdivisions, on golf courses, and as part of flood control and water recharge projects. These lakes and ponds are a magnet for birds. They provide some of the area's best birding, especially during the winter months, when they attract a variety of wintering ducks, geese, and other waterbirds.

On any given day during the winter, it's not at all difficult to find 10 to 12 different duck species on these waters. The area's lakes and ponds have also hosted a number of rare and unusual species, including the state's first Tufted Duck, which showed up at a small pond in the east valley. Its first Glaucous Gull was spotted at an urban lake in Scottsdale, a Black-legged Kittiwake visited a subdivision pond in Chandler, and a Yellow-billed Loon and Red-necked Grebe were found at Tempe Town Lake. Most Arizona birders have seen their life Eurasian Wigeon at a lake or pond in the Scottsdale area, where they are usually found in large flocks of wintering American Wigeons.

Birding Arizona

Canada Geese are fun to watch and easy to find at many ponds and lakes in the area. Some of these geese now stay year-round. Rare and unusual goose species can sometimes be found in wintering flocks of Canada Geese, including an occasional Snow, Ross's and White-fronted Goose, as well as the hard-to-identify Cackling Goose (a newly named species that looks like a very small version of the Canada Goose and is about the size of a Mallard).

During spring and fall landbird migration, interesting birds can be found just about any place you find trees. For example, one of my favorite places to look for fall migrants in early September is in the mesquite trees along the Indian Bend Wash greenbelt in Scottsdale, next to a small skateboard park. Some September mornings have yielded an impressive list of migrating flycatchers, vireos, and warblers, including Wilson's, Nashville, Orange-crowned, Black-throated Gray, MacGillivray's, and Lucy's. One fall, a Blackburnian Warbler was found in this area and stayed around for several days to be enjoyed by many local birders. All this bird activity takes place only a few hundred yards from one of the busiest intersections in the Phoenix metropolitan area. In downtown Phoenix, mesquite and ornamental trees next to City Hall have attracted a variety of rare birds over the years, including Prothonotary Warbler, Varied Thrush, and even a Rufous-backed Robin.

Rare vagrant and migrant species are sometimes found in urban locations in very unusual places. For example, I saw my first state Ovenbird walking about in the well of an orange tree in a yard in Phoenix, my first state Kentucky Warbler hopping alongside a Phoenix swimming pool, and my first state Worm-eating Warbler atop a fence in a Tempe backyard.

Chapter 4

For hawk watchers, the Phoenix metropolitan area can be very productive. Harris's Hawks seem to be adapting to our urban environment and can be found nesting in tall trees. Also watch for American Kestrel and Cooper's and Red-tailed hawks. In downtown Phoenix, Peregrine Falcons are sometimes seen perched on tall buildings, from which they hunt Rock Pigeons.

Look and listen for night birds, even in the city. Great Horned Owls are fairly common permanent residents in our urban areas. They can often be seen perched on power poles or even sitting on rooftops and chimneys. Beginning with the onset of their breeding season in midwinter, their low distinctive "who's awake, me too" calls are often heard in residential areas. In parts of the city—especially where there are saguaro cactus—you can sometimes hear Western Screech Owls giving their distinctive bouncing-ball-like calls. We sometimes forget that many owl species are migratory. Phoenix's Desert Botanical Garden has hosted a number of migrating owls over the years, including Flammulated, Long-eared, and Northern Saw-whet. In summertime near dusk, look up in the sky and you can often see Lesser Nighthawks flying through the gathering darkness.

Rosy-faced Lovebirds are an introduced exotic species that birders in the Phoenix metropolitan area now find with regularity. Native to southwestern Africa, they've become established local breeders. In 2012, they were officially added to the American Ornithological Union's checklist. Birders come from around the country to add them to their life lists. These small parrots have a rosy-red throat and face, green body, and short bluish-colored tail. They are often found in older, more established neighborhoods, where they roost and nest in mature deciduous trees and tall palms.

Birding Arizona

Encanto Park in downtown Phoenix is, perhaps, the most reliable place to see them. They are noisy and easy to find.

I recently did an informal survey by asking birding friends what they consider the best birding spots in the Phoenix metropolitan area. There was near-unanimous agreement about the top four: the Gilbert Water Ranch, Desert Botanical Garden, Tres Rios, and the Glendale Recharge Ponds.

The Riparian Preserve at Water Ranch in the suburb of Gilbert (better known as the Gilbert Water Ranch) is a 100-acre facility consisting of seven recharge basins. These ponds are connected by over four miles of trails through desert and riparian habitats. Water levels in the ponds vary from time to time, and in summer, some ponds can be completely dry. Over 280 bird species have been reported from this area. It's easily reached by freeway, and much of the area is accessible to people with disabilities.

Among the many rare and unusual species found at Gilbert Water Ranch are numerous eastern vagrant warblers, including Tennessee, Magnolia, Blackpoll, Prairie, American Redstart, and Northern Parula. No less impressive has been the number of rare shorebirds, gulls, terns, herons, and other waterbirds dropping in for a visit, including Ruff, Short-billed Dowitcher, Purple Gallinule, Sabine's Gull, Least and Elegant terns, and Wood Stork, to name just a few.

In winter, the recharge basins host hundreds of ducks. Perhaps the most outstanding bird found here was a Baikal Teal. It was discovered with a group of other teal species in November 2009. Birders came from around the country to see this rare duck, which breeds in eastern Siberia and winters in Asia. This remarkable record has been officially accepted by the Arizona Bird Committee.

A particularly productive place to look for desert-dwelling species in Phoenix is the Desert Botanical Garden, which regularly conducts bird walks. Located on 140 acres of beautiful Sonoran Desert in the heart of the city, it displays rare and threatened desert flora from around the world, as well as a range of native desert plant species.

The garden is a birder's paradise. Its blooming plants, abundant trees, small pond, and flower gardens attract both nesting and wintering birds, as well as migrating species in spring and fall. It is famous for its hummingbirds, which are attracted to flower species such as fairy duster, chuparosa, and various penstemons. Look for Anna's, Costa's, Black-chinned, and occasional Rufous hummingbirds in migration.

The Desert Botanical Garden is a reliable place to find such desert-nesting species as White-winged Dove, Gambel's Quail, Gila Woodpecker, Curve-billed Thrasher, Verdin, Black-tailed Gnatcatcher, Phainopepla, Ash-throated Flycatcher, and that iconic bird of the American Southwest, the Greater Roadrunner. A bird that is hard to miss here is Abert's Towhee, a desert species that has successfully colonized much of urban Phoenix. A very sedentary bird, this large sparrow is almost an Arizona endemic species, with a very large percentage of its range restricted to the Grand Canyon State. Abert's Towhees can often be observed on the ground, scratching under leaves and vegetation in a hunt for insects and seeds.

If you want to watch and study marsh and other water birds, there is no better place to do it than the Tres Rios Wetlands southwest of Phoenix. At Tres Rios, water from flow-regulating ponds drops into an overbank wetland of dense cattails and emergent vegetation. You can follow this ribbon of marsh and riparian vegetation interspersed with open water and ponds for over two miles along a gravel roadway.

Tres Rios is home to a variety of birds commonly associated with marshes, including such species as Red-winged and Yellow-headed blackbirds, Yellowthroat, American Coot, and Common Gallinule. It's a wonderful place to learn the songs and calls of such hard-to-see marsh inhabitants as Sora, Virginia Rail, Least Bittern, Pied-billed Grebe, and Marsh Wren. As you walk along, keep an eye out for Great Blue and Green herons, Least Bittern, and Great and Snowy egrets. Other waterbirds often found here in proper season include Cinnamon and Blue-winged teals, Black-bellied Whistling Duck, and White-faced Ibis.

Good shorebird habitat is hard to find in Arizona. The Glendale Recharge Ponds in the northwest part of the valley are perhaps the premier shorebirding spot in Arizona. During fall shorebird migration, which begins in early July, there is almost a constant turnover of migrating shorebirds. During peak migration toward the end of August, shorebirders can often find 15 to 20 different shorebird species. Some of the rarer shorebirds found here include Red Knot, Ruff, Semipalmated Sandpiper, and American Golden Plover. The Glendale Recharge Ponds are also a great place to look for gulls, terns, raptors, and wintering ducks. A permit is required to visit the area and can easily be obtained by calling (602) 495-7477.

Some of my other favorite spots to watch birds in the

Phoenix metropolitan area include South Mountain Park, Veteran's Oasis Park, the Rio Salado Habitat Restoration Area, and Tempe Town Lake. Best of all, with a little effort, you can find your own "patch" for watching and enjoying birds in this urban environment.

For a list and description of other birding locations in the Phoenix metropolitan area and Maricopa County, consult the current edition of *Birds of Phoenix and Maricopa County*, published by the Maricopa Audubon Society.

Directions to Phoenix Metropolitan Area Birding Hot Spots:

Desert Botanical Garden

(in north Phoenix) Located in Papago Park, at 1201 N. Galvin Parkway.

Gilbert Water Ranch

(southeast of Phoenix, in Gilbert) From eastbound US 60, turn right on Greenfield Road (exit 185) and drive south 1.5 miles. Turn left (east) on Guadalupe Road. The entrance is the third driveway on the right.

Tres Rios Wetlands

(southwest of Phoenix) Go west on Interstate 10 to the 91st Avenue exit, and go south for 5 miles. At about 5 miles, you will see the fenced wetlands on the right. Continue south on 91st Avenue to the end of the fence, where there is a parking area.

Glendale Recharge Ponds

(northwest of Phoenix, in Glendale) Take Camelback Road west from Loop 101 for 1.2 miles. Turn right and go north on 107th Avenue. Continue north on 107th Avenue all the way to the dead end. Continue straight ahead and park on the bridge over the drainage channel at the southwest corner of the ponds. You can also follow the dirt road (which is actually Bethany Home Road) that turns off sharply to the right (east). Continue on this dirt road until you reach the end, where stone walls prevent any further driving east. Park here and walk into the southeast corner of the ponds.

San Francisco Peaks

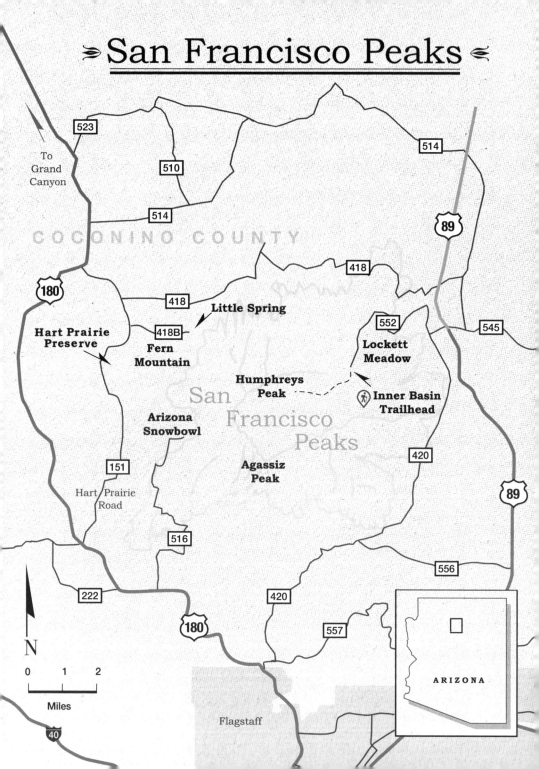

523

To
Grand
Canyon

510

514

514

COCONINO COUNTY

89

180

418

418

Little Spring

Hart Prairie
Preserve

418B

Fern
Mountain

552

545

Lockett
Meadow

Humphreys
Peak

Inner Basin
Trailhead

Arizona
Snowbowl

San
Francisco
Peaks

420

151

Hart Prairie
Road

Agassiz
Peak

516

556

222

420

89

N

0   1   2

Miles

180

557

40

ARIZONA

Flagstaff

Chapter 4

Birding the San Francisco Peaks

If you want to get out of the summer heat and find a cool, refreshing spot to go birding, the San Francisco Peaks north of Flagstaff fit the bill perfectly. "The Peaks," as they're often called, are one of the dominant geologic features of the Colorado Plateau. Rising to nearly 13,000 feet, they are the remnants of an old Fujiyama-style stratovolcano that once towered over 15,000 feet. Violent eruptions, collapse, glaciers, and erosion all helped shape the present-day peaks, which were formed from the rim of the old volcano. Their summits, snowcapped for much of the year, are a landmark that can be seen over a hundred miles away.

Hart Prairie, along the west side of the peaks, is a great place to look for birds—especially the area around the Hart Prairie Preserve. This area was purchased by The Nature Conservancy in 1994, in part to protect a rare Bebb willow community. These tree-sized willows are scattered about the property, but many are concentrated along a small, intermittent stream that runs along the base of Fern Mountain, a low volcanic hill whose slopes are covered in the summer by dense bracken ferns.

Two bird species that breed very locally in Arizona can often be found along the base of Fern Mountain—Orange-crowned Warbler and Dusky Flycatcher. Listen for their songs and chip notes as you walk through the willows. Be careful, however. The Orange-crowned Warbler's song can be mistaken for the dry, mechanical trill of the Chipping Sparrow, which also breeds in the area.

Other, more common breeding species seen here include Western Tanager, Black-headed Grosbeak, Green-tailed Towhee, and Mountain Bluebird. On summer evenings, you can sometimes hear the booming courtship sound of Common Nighthawks and the soft repetitious hooting of Flammulated Owls. The road near the preserve provides stunning views of Humphreys and Agassiz peaks. The area is particularly beautiful in the fall, when aspen groves turn golden yellow.

A bit farther up the Hart Prairie Road (FR 151), you can visit Little Spring. Turn on FR 418(B) and follow it about a half mile to a closed gate, where you can park. Then walk along the road a few hundred yards to a large meadow. The spring is tucked away at the top of the meadow, near the base of the mountain on the right. Here, spring water trickles out of a pipe and collects in a pool, surrounded by large gooseberry bushes. This is perhaps one of the most idyllic and beautiful birding spots in Arizona.

In 1889, the C. Hart Merriam expedition camped at Little Spring. From very early on, the San Francisco Peaks attracted the attention of naturalists and people interested in the area's bird life. Merriam was chief of ornithology and mammology at the Smithsonian Institution. That year, he was sent to do a general biological survey of the San Francisco mountains region. Using Little Spring as their base, Merriam's expedition made several reconnaissance trips to the nearby Painted Desert and Grand Canyon.

It was while he was camped at Little Spring that Merriam gathered information for his famous "life zones" concept of vegetative distribution. He hypothesized that plant and animal communities yielded to one another along an elevational gradient based primarily on temperature. Belts of plant and animal communities would be similarly expressed with an increase in altitude or latitude. He broke these communities down into distinct life zones and gave them names, many of which should sound familiar to birders. They include the alpine, Hudsonian, Canadian and pine zones, all of which he encountered as he surveyed from the bottom to the top of the San Francisco Peaks. Although much of his life zone theory has now been supplanted, Merriam's life zone classifications have been followed by biologists and writers up to recent times. Two of the many books that employed these classifications are *The Birds of Arizona* (Phillips) and *A Field Guide to the Plants of Arizona* (Epple).

Merriam's expedition included Dr. Leonhard Stejneger, curator of reptiles at the US National Museum, a famous naturalist and scientist in his own right. Stejneger should be familiar to birders as the person for whom Stejneger's Petrel—a sea bird often looked for on pelagic trips off the West Coast—is named.

At Little Spring, the birding is often just as good as the scenery is lovely. Another very locally breeding bird, MacGillivray's Warbler, can often be found in the gooseberry bushes near the spring. A little "pishing" will sometimes get one of these handsome warblers to pop into view. The forested slopes around the spring, clad in spruces and firs, are an excellent place to look for such species as Red-faced Warbler, Red-breasted Nuthatch, and Mountain Chickadee. An impressive number of eastern variant species have been found here near the spring, including Kentucky Warbler, American Redstart, Chestnut-sided Warbler, and Gray Catbird. Evening Grosbeak is a very erratic and uncommon breeder in Arizona, but it seems to nest in this area with some frequency.

Birding Arizona

Band-tailed Pigeon is an often-overlooked species that can be found in summer around Little Spring. You sometimes see these large pigeons perched in pine snags or hear them as they flush from conifers. Most often, you hear Band-tailed Pigeons before you see them. Their wings make a loud and distinct "whap whap whap" sound as they fly from a perch. They also give a low "whoo whoo" call that can fool inexperienced birders into thinking they're hearing an owl. When they flush, these pigeons (like their city cousins) often fly around in a circle before landing again.

The Band-tailed Pigeon nests in coniferous forests in the Pacific Northwest, and in oak and conifer woodlands in the Southwest. Arizona birds are of the interior southwestern race. They migrate to Mexico in autumn, returning here to nest in April. In winter, they can often be found in numbers in the barrancas along the Sinaloa-Durango border in Mexico. I fondly remember watching a flock of these beautiful pigeons in a pine snag in the Barranca Rancho Liebre in Durango while searching for Mexico's famous Tufted Jay.

Little Spring is also a good place to look for sapsuckers, both Williamson's and Red-naped. These woodpeckers are often found in aspen groves. Female Williamson's Sapsuckers look nothing like the striking males with their black, red, yellow, and white plumage. The females have a brown head and barred back and look something like a flicker. In fact, they look so different from males of their own species that for a long time, they were thought to be a separate species and were actually named the Black-breasted Woodpecker. The trees around Little Spring often reveal sapsucker wells drilled into the trunks in neat parallel rows. I have seen migrating Rufous Hummingbirds sipping the sap from these wells to fuel up during their long migration.

The first naturalist to climb to the top of the San Francisco Peaks was Dr. Edgar A. Mearns, who climbed them in the summer of 1887, two years before the arrival of the C. Hart Merriam expedition. Mearns, like so many early southwestern naturalists, was an army doctor. In 1884, he accompanied General George Crook to the Havasupai Indian village at the bottom of the Grand Canyon and also traveled extensively in the mountainous regions of central Arizona. A physician by training, he was also a passionate ornithologist and collector, one of the founders of the American Ornithologists' Union. On his climb to the top of the peaks, he reportedly collected a Northern Goshawk near the timberline. Mearns was the first ornithologist to find a Northern Saw-whet Owl nest in Arizona, which he also discovered on the peaks.

For birders who would like to follow in Dr. Mearns's footsteps to the top of the peaks, it can be an exhilarating and rewarding, albeit strenuous, experience. On the east side of the peaks, you can hike up into the Inner Basin by following the Inner Basin Trail from Lockett Meadow. This hike leads through beautiful scenery up into the "caldera" or heart of the old volcano. Sometimes, you can flush a Dusky Grouse on the way up. A small transplanted population of these game birds seems to have become well established on the peaks. They like openings in the forest where bushes like dwarf juniper, gooseberry, and raspberry grow.

Perhaps the easiest and most direct way to the top of the peaks is to take the Humphreys Peak Trail, which starts at the Arizona Snowbowl ski area. For the first two miles, you walk through a dense mixed-conifer forest. Most of the trees are Douglas-fir and

Engelmann spruce. In this area, listen for the snappy two-syllable calls of the Cordilleran Flycatcher, and watch for boreal species like Golden-crowned Kinglet, Red Crossbill, Steller's Jay, and Clark's Nutcracker. You'll often hear the one-note call of the Brown Creeper, which is very similar to the high-pitched notes of the Golden-crowned Kinglet. Brown Creepers often begin singing very early in springtime. Their lively up-and-down bouncy song can be heard at the Arizona Snowbowl as early as March, even when there is still five feet of snow on the ground.

As you climb up the trail, listen for the ethereal voice of the Hermit Thrush. Theodore Roosevelt once described this song as the "sweetest sound of the wilderness." There are historical records of breeding Swainson's Thrush on the San Francisco Peaks, although there are no recent reports. Still, I always listen for their rising, flute-like songs when hiking the area in summertime.

As you climb higher, the trees thin out. At about 10,000 feet, or three and a half miles up the trail, you begin to see bristlecone pine trees. These gnarled and twisted pines are about the only tree species that can survive the snow, cold, and wind at this altitude. The San Francisco Peaks are the only place in Arizona where they grow. Tree ring analysis revealed the age of one of these bristlecone pines to be 1,400 years. I have seen Clark's Nutcrackers near the timberline collecting pine seeds in these trees.

Two bird species that breed nowhere else in Arizona can sometimes be found near or above the timberline—American Pipit and White-crowned Sparrow. The pipits and sparrows nest at around 11,000 feet elevation on volcanic talus slopes that are covered with subalpine conifer scrublands also known as "krumm-

132

holtz" or "elfinwoods." Sometimes, the pipits can be heard flying overhead, giving their "pi-pit" call. Both species may also breed on top of Mount Baldy, in the White Mountains.

Near the summit, the footing is difficult, with loose volcanic rock and jagged lava underfoot. Rock Wrens are often seen and heard near the summit. For some reason, I'm always surprised to see them, not because there are not plenty of rocks, but because I associate these wrens with rocky desert habitat. Another bird almost always found up near the summit is the Common Raven. As they fly by turning, twisting, and gliding in updrafts along the ridges, their acrobatics are a joy to watch.

The vegetation at the top of the peaks is unique and includes some rare alpine flora. Among the plants is an endangered species found nowhere else—the San Francisco Peaks groundsel. This small, daisy-like plant, with crinkly leaves and yellow flowers, grows low to the ground among the lava rocks and boulders. The alpine vegetation or tundra at the top of the peaks is geographically isolated, much like an island. This increases the chances that endemic species like the groundsel will evolve. Another example of this can be seen with the geographically isolated Kaibab Squirrel, which inhabits the Kaibab Plateau on the North Rim of the Grand Canyon. As you look out to the north from the top of Humphreys Peak, you can make out the North Rim—that will be our next birding destination.

⇝ Kaibab Plateau ⇜

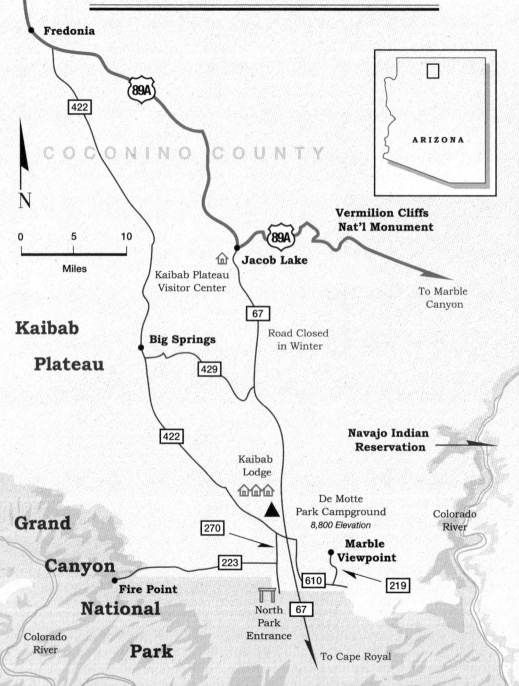

Fredonia

89A

422

COCONINO COUNTY

ARIZONA

N

0   5   10

Miles

Vermilion Cliffs
Nat'l Monument

89A

Jacob Lake

Kaibab Plateau
Visitor Center

To Marble
Canyon

67

Kaibab

Road Closed
in Winter

Plateau

Big Springs

429

422

Navajo Indian
Reservation

Kaibab
Lodge

De Motte
Park Campground
8,800 Elevation

Colorado
River

Grand

270

**Marble
Viewpoint**

Canyon

223

610

219

Fire Point

National

North
Park
Entrance

67

Colorado
River

Park

To Cape Royal

Chapter 4

Birding the Kaibab Plateau

American Three-toed Woodpecker, Dusky Grouse, Evening Grosbeak, Cassin's Finch, and Northern Goshawk are just some of the sought-after species to be found in the conifer forests of northern Arizona's Kaibab Plateau. Besides outstanding birding, the plateau offers visitors incomparable scenery, with stunning views of the Grand Canyon from forested points and overlooks along the canyon's North Rim.

The Kaibab Plateau is divided into two parts; the southern third, which is in Grand Canyon National Park, and the northern two-thirds, which is part of the Kaibab National Forest. The starting point for a visit to this area is Jacob Lake. (It should be noted that most of the dirt forest roads on the plateau, including the ones mentioned in this section, are well maintained and can be driven in standard passenger cars.)

From Jacob Lake, Arizona State Route 67 winds south through a ponderosa pine forest interspersed with large stands of aspen trees. At about 10 miles, you travel through a large burned area. You'll notice that many young aspen trees have regenerated here and in other fire-burned areas on the plateau.

At about 15 miles, you begin traveling along beautiful blue spruce–lined "parks." Swainson's and Red-tailed hawks can sometimes be seen in these large mountain meadows. At about 25 miles, you see the Kaibab Lodge on your right. The entrance to DeMotte Campground is a few hundred yards farther on, also on your right. The elevation is about 8,800 feet. Here you'll begin an adventure that will take you through some of the most beautiful scenery and exciting birding that Arizona can offer.

DeMotte Campground is a good central location from which to fan out and begin birding and exploring the area. The forest around the campground is one of the best places on the plateau to see many of its boreal species, including the American Three-toed Woodpecker. Look for them along the forested park edge just south of the campground. You can often find them by listening for their tapping sounds and looking for trees they have been working. Three-toed Woodpeckers peel and flake the bark off trees, looking for insects. You can sometimes spot trees with large patches of flaked-off bark and piles of bark platelets on the ground.

The forest near this campground is also a reliable place to look for other boreal species, such as Red Crossbill, Evening Grosbeak, Golden-crowned Kinglet, Clark's Nutcracker, Northern Pygmy-Owl, and Northern Saw-whet Owl. Other species that frequent the area include Williamson's Sapsucker, Mountain Bluebird, and Red-breasted Nuthatch. All three Arizona nuthatches—White-breasted, Pygmy, and Red-breasted—can be found here. Around the campground, there are always a number of Dark-eyed Juncos. The juncos on the North Rim are mostly of the Red-backed form of the Dark-eyed Junco (also called the Gray-headed Junco, *dorsalsi* spp). They are distinguished by a bicolored bill.

DeMotte Campground is also a good place to see Cassin's Finch, whose Arizona breeding range is restricted to the Kaibab Plateau and a few remote areas in the northeastern part of the state. They are easy to view at the feeders that are sometimes set out at the country store across from the campground, or at feeders and a fountain at Jacob Lake. At dusk, look for occasional flocks of Wild Turkeys, which move into the park to feed. The plateau has a large turkey population, and you can run into them just about anywhere. These are Merriam's Turkeys, a different race than those found in the mountains of southeastern Arizona.

Take some time to look at the stars if you go out looking for a Northern Saw-whet Owl. When you gaze up at the summer sky on a dark and cloudless night, constellations like Scorpio, Cassiopeia, and the dippers seem to hang almost within reach. This is no doubt due to the plateau's exceptionally clear atmosphere, high elevation, and lack of light pollution.

The Dusky Grouse is one of Arizona's most sought-after bird species. Once considered a subspecies of the Blue Grouse, it is now recognized as a separate species. A very reliable place to find them is along the road to Marble Viewpoint, the turnoff to which is just south of DeMotte Park. The road to Marble Viewpoint, like many on the plateau, is lined with New Mexico locust, a large shrub that produces beautiful bright-pink blossoms in early summer. As you drive to the overlook, watch for grouse, especially along canyon rims, from which they fly out when startled. Also look for them in clearings with gooseberry and common juniper bushes. As you drive along, keep an eye out for Band-tailed Pigeon, Hairy Woodpecker, Northern Flicker, and Green-tailed Towhee.

"Breathtaking" is the only word that can describe the scenery from Marble Viewpoint's forested and windswept overlook. After summer monsoon rains, the ground around Marble Viewpoint can blaze with Indian paintbrush, Cooper's goldenflower, and purple aster. As you look east, you can see House Rock Valley and the Vermilion Cliffs in the foreground. The Vermilion Cliffs are the Arizona release site of endangered California Condors. Watch for them just about anywhere on the Kaibab Plateau.

The large, rounded mountain you see on the far horizon is Navajo Mountain, a heavily forested volcanic laccolith that, at 10,500 feet, is the highest point on Navajo tribal lands. To the right of Navajo Mountain stretch the vast lands of the Navajo and Hopi, which we'll explore in the next section.

As you return to DeMotte Campground, stop occasionally and look and listen for flocks of birds moving through the aspen groves. These are often mixed flocks that may include such species as Mountain Chickadee, Pygmy and White-breasted nuthatches, Yellow-rumped Warbler, Brown Creeper, House Wren, Ruby-crowned Kinglet, Warbling Vireo, and others.

Another beautiful spot to look for birds is Fire Point, which is a 13-mile drive from DeMotte Park along well-marked and frequently traveled roads. Driving toward Fire Point, you might catch a glimpse of a Northern Goshawk. The Kaibab Plateau is thought to have once harbored the densest population of these large accipiters in North America. Heavy commercial logging on the Kaibab National Forest during the 1980s and 1990s caused severe habitat fragmentation and loss of tree canopy closure that threatens not only the Northern Goshawk, but other old-growth-dependent species, such as Kaibab squirrel, Flammulated Owl, and Sharp-shinned Hawk.

As you approach Fire Point, you notice more and more big, yellow-barked ponderosa pines. The bark on these trees does not begin to turn yellow until the tree is around 150 years old. On Fire

Point, you find yourself in the middle of a magnificent stand of old-growth trees. This is how the plateau's pine forests once looked, before many of the big trees were cut and large areas reduced to ugly, unregenerated clearcuts. The last mile of the road to the overlook winds through these large trees. At the point, you discover a magnificent view of the Grand Canyon looking east toward Great Thumb Mesa. Look carefully and you can make out some beautiful amphitheaters in the rock formations across the canyon.

Birding Fire Point can be very productive. In the big pines, watch for the Downy Woodpecker. The Kaibab Plateau is one of the best places in Arizona to find this small, white-backed woodpecker. The similar-looking Hairy Woodpecker is also found here. Also watch for Acorn Woodpecker, Williamson's Sapsucker, Evening and Black-headed grosbeaks, and Red Crossbill. During migration, watch for Hermit and Townsend's warblers. During the day, listen for Northern Pygmy-Owl, and at night for Common Poorwill. In the chaparral on the point's south side, look for Ash-throated Flycatcher, Virginia's Warbler, Spotted Towhee, and Lesser Goldfinch. In late summer, the purple and red blooms of Wheeler's thistle and skyrocket gilia attract Broad-tailed, Rufous, and occasionally Calliope hummingbirds.

The big pines at Fire Point are also an easy place to see the plateau's most famous mammal, the Kaibab squirrel. This beautiful tassel-eared squirrel has evolved an all-white tail, unlike the white-and-gray tail of its relative, the Abert's squirrel, which lives on the south side of the Grand Canyon. This example of divergent evolution reminds us that the Kaibab Plateau, like many southwestern forests, is an isolated forest ecosystem that is both unique and highly vulnerable to human activity and disturbance.

While on the plateau, you will want to visit Grand Canyon National Park. Because of steeper canyon drainages and more restricted access, birding inside the park is not as easy as in the Kaibab National Forest. However, there are a number of excellent birding spots.

From DeMotte Park, drive four miles south on State Route 67 to the park entrance, where you pay a fee. Once inside the national park, one of my favorite places to bird is Cape Royal. Its location in pinyon-juniper habitat gives you a different suite of birds to look for. As you walk out to the canyon rim, watch for Gray Flycatcher, Spotted Towhee, Black-throated Gray Warbler, Juniper Titmouse, Bushtit, and Woodhouse's Scrub Jay. White-throated Swifts often fly through the canyon, making a swooshing sound with their wings.

Another nice spot to stop and bird in the national park is Greenland Lake, on the way to Point Imperial. Try walking the trail that circles this small body of water. You can find many of the boreal species already mentioned, including Evening Grosbeak and Steller's Jay.

Another interesting spot to look for some different species and wrap up your tour of the Kaibab Plateau is Big Springs, a Forest Service work camp about 23 miles from DeMotte Park. Big Springs is located in a north-south canyon on the north side of the plateau. It gets its name from the large spring that flows out of the Coconino Sandstone formation on the canyon's east wall. The water runs into two large ponds on the property, which are stocked with trout. The area has a mix of non-native and native trees and bushes. Ask permission to enter and bird the area around the ponds, including two very large willow trees. Look for Western Kingbird, Yellow Warbler, and Bullock's Oriole. MacGillivray's Warbler, which breeds very locally, can often be found in the tangled brushy area just north of the ponds. In weedy areas, look for Chipping, Vesper, Brewer's, and Lark sparrows.

Try birding the riparian vegetation along the roadside north of the Big Springs work camp. Look for Townsend's Solitaire, Grace's Warbler, Western Tanager, and Indigo Bunting. The sides of the canyon north of the work camp are pine and pinyon-juniper habitat. Listen for raucous flocks of Pinyon Jays and the beautiful descending song of Canyon Wrens. At night, this is a good place to hear Flammulated Owls and Western Screech-Owls. Big Springs is a great place to check for migrants, especially in the fall, as they funnel up through the canyon attracted to the area's lush vegetation and water. Among the birds to look for in migration are Townsend's, Hermit, Nashville, Virginia's, and Black-throated Gray warblers. The North Rim is a marvelous place to bird, whether in summer when the New Mexico locust is blooming, or in fall when the aspens have turned to gold.

Northeastern Arizona

Lake Powell

Colorado River

Page

98

Navaho Nation Reservation

163

Kayenta

191

COCONINO COUNTY

59

Cow Springs Lake

Tonalea Gas Station/Store

160

Many Farms Lake

NAVAHO COUNTY

Chinle

Canyon de Chelly

Tuba City

Pasture Canyon

264

APACHE COUNTY

Cameron

Keams Canyon

27

Gray Mountain

Hubbell Trading Post

Ganado Lake

Ganado

264

89

Hopi Nation Reservation

15

Greasewood

Little Colorado River

87

40

Flagstaff

40

77

17

87

Holbrook

ARIZONA

0   10   20

Miles

N

Chapter 4

Chasing Rarities Across Northeastern Arizona

A trip to the northeastern part of Arizona in the spring or fall to look for rare migrant and vagrant birds is one of Arizona's great birding experiences. Much of this vast area is Navajo and Hopi tribal lands, which together comprise nearly 15 percent of the state's total land area.

Scattered and dispersed across these tribal lands are "migrant traps," oases of trees and water that attract migrating and vagrant birds. Birding conditions at these traps can change from one year to the next. A place that is a watery green oasis one year can be completely dried up 12 months later—and vice versa. In short: where you find water, you find birds.

The area can be roughly divided into two parts: the eastern Navajo Nation and the western Navajo Nation. Within the latter is the much smaller Hopi Reservation, which encompasses more than 1.5 million acres and is made up of 12 villages on three mesas. Northeastern Arizona is a land of magnificent scenery—carved sandstone canyons, towering monuments, volcanic buttes, and juniper-covered plateaus and mesas. Towns and settlements are few and far between, roads can be poorly marked, and accommodations sometimes difficult to find. However, for the birder with a sense of adventure who is willing to get off the beaten path and do some exploring, it can be a rewarding and unforgettable experience.

Birding Arizona

The Eastern Navajo Nation

Ganado, Arizona, is a good starting place to explore the eastern tribal lands of the Navajo. This small community is famous for the beautiful "Ganado Red" rugs woven by local Navajo women. Just north of town on Navajo 27 is Ganado Lake, one of the area's best and most productive birding spots.

On spring and fall birding trips to this area, we often arrive at Ganado Lake late at night, just in time to throw our sleeping bags on the ground under large willows along the shore. We fall asleep listening to the distant barking of Navajo dogs and the calls of American Wigeons out on the water. Over the years, many interesting migrant and vagrant birds have been found here, including Palm Warbler, Eastern Kingbird, and Red-eyed Vireo. One fall, a wandering Little Blue Heron arrived at Ganado Lake and stayed for several weeks. In springtime, it is a very reliable place to see migrating gulls, the most common of which are Ring-billed, California, Bonaparte's, and Franklin's, as well as migrating Forster's Terns and an occasional Black Tern. It can also attract shorebirds. One spring, we found a Red Phalarope on the water, and on another occasion, a Sanderling in breeding plumage, forced down by fierce spring winds. The Sanderling had us scratching our heads for a while. In Arizona's autumn months, Sanderlings are mostly found in non-breeding plumage; rarely do you see the bird in its beautiful breeding plumage.

Just west of Ganado on Highway 264 is the old Hubbell Trading Post, a national historic site situated on the bank of Ganado Wash. Built in 1878, it is the oldest continually operated trading post in the Southwest. It holds a wonderful collection of old rugs and art, and taking a tour of the site is well worth the time. Outside, picnic tables are set out under tall cottonwood trees whose leaves turn golden yellow in autumn. It's a tranquil place, perfect for breaking out a can of sardines and a box of crackers for lunch.

The large cottonwoods are a nice place to spend time birding. Some rarer species found here include Baltimore Oriole, American Redstart, and Rose-breasted Grosbeak. In spring, Pine Siskin, American and Lesser goldfinches, and Lazuli and Indigo buntings can often be seen feeding on catkins high up in the trees.

Ganado Wash was once one of the area's best birding spots. The dense thickets of Russian olive and tamarisk upstream from the highway produced many rare species, such as Northern Parula, Blackpoll Warbler, Hooded Warbler, Eastern Phoebe, and Northern Waterthrush. During the cold winter months, they provided cover and food for Cassin's Finch, Evening Grosbeak, and the occasional White-throated or Harris's sparrows. Today, however, most if not all this vegetation has been cut and cleared. The hope is that by removing the Russian olive and tamarisk, native vegetation like cottonwood and willow will become reestablished. Of these two exotics, Russian olive is probably a little less undesirable. It has mean, shirt-ripping thorns, but its grainy fruits sustain flocks of birds in winter, and its flowers scent the air on windy spring evenings.

From Ganado, visiting birders often travel north along US 191 across the Defiance Plateau to Chinle, Arizona. Travel in this part of Arizona can sometimes be a lonely experience, especially in wintertime. I particularly remember a trip a number of years ago. A biologist friend called to tell me he'd found a small flock of American Tree Sparrows in a field along Chinle Wash. I left Phoenix late, driving through Holbrook and then north to Bidahochi, where Navajo 15 turns east toward the lower part of the community of Greasewood. It was a crystal-clear, moonless night with temperatures around 15 degrees. For the next 80 miles, I never saw another vehicle.

Chinle is in the heart of Navajo tribal lands. It is also the jumping-off point for visits to Canyon de Chelly National Monument. The Thunderbird Lodge at the mouth of Canyon de Chelly got its start as a trading post in 1902. Cool, well-watered lawns and trees around the lodge offer a pleasant contrast to the surrounding area's harsh plateaus and mesas. The lodge's cafeteria serves hot meals. No visit to this part of Arizona is complete until you eat a Navajo taco. This famous local dish is made of "frybread," a thick unyeasted bread, topped with chili beans, covered with grated onions and cheese, and topped again with strips of green chile and spoonfuls of salsa.

The area around the lodge is well worth birding, especially in springtime. Cedar Waxwings are usually found in the trees, giving their busy call notes, and American Robins are always hopping about on the lawn looking for earthworms. Watch for Bullock's Orioles, which nest in the tall cottonwoods. In the fall, there are records of Eastern Kingbird, one of my favorite eastern vagrants. They are usually found in late August or early September.

About 15 miles north of Chinle on US 191 is Many Farms Lake, a large reservoir that irrigates nearby farms and ranches. Its size and location make this lake a magnet for unusual birds, especially waterbirds like ducks, geese, and gulls. Behind the lake, the steep walls of Round Rock Butte rise up in the background. Its shape reminds me of the "mittens" in Monument Valley, the famous backdrop for many John Ford movies of the 1940s and 1950s.

Birding Many Farms Lake can be difficult. To get close to the birds, you often have to walk through mud, ford small streams, and zigzag through cornfields. Worst of all, you have to cross barbed-wire fences. These become more challenging with age. When I was younger, I could cross by pulling up on the third strand, stepping down on the second, bending my back, and stooping under. Now, I look up and down the fence line for a sturdy post where the strands are tightly wired. I can climb up and over more easily there, hoping the wires won't give way. Small holes and tears in my faded jeans are proof that they usually do.

The water level of Many Farms Lake fluctuates with the seasons. The best birding is usually along its shoreline, where there is always a large swath of cocklebur. Dozens of spiny, irritating burs cling to pant legs and worm their way into socks and shoes as you walk along. One spring morning in 1987, we found a White-rumped Sandpiper standing in flooded cocklebur. At the time, it was only the second recorded sighting in Arizona. The White-rumped Sandpiper is a tundra breeder that winters at the tip of South America. Its usual spring migration route is through the central and eastern parts of the continent.

A variety of waterbirds have been found at Many Farms Lake—everything from Herring Gull and Tundra Swan to Ross's Goose and Surf Scoter. This spot is regularly visited in migration by flocks of American White Pelicans that breed in the Great Basin, and there is even a record of a wandering Brown Pelican.

The lake's shoreline has produced many interesting shorebirds, including American Golden-Plover, Black-bellied Plover, Sanderling, Semipalmated Sandpiper, Short-billed Dowitcher, and Whimbrel. The shorebirding, however, is always unpredictable because of fluctuating water levels. In years when winter runoff is good, the water gets backed up into the surrounding vegetation, leaving little if any suitable shorebird habitat.

For many years, Many Farms Lake was one of a handful of places in Arizona to find Black-billed Magpies. They could be seen or heard giving their loud "mag, mag" calls around the large cottonwood trees on the lake's east side. They have not been found for several years now, and it is believed that the small population may have been wiped out by West Nile virus.

Traveling west from Ganado on Highway 264, you can visit Keams Canyon, an often-overlooked and under-birded spot on the eastern edge of the Hopi Reservation. Keams Canyon is an administrative center for the Bureau of Indian Affairs, with a number of government buildings, a school, and a store. The canyon is about eight miles long, with extensive riparian cottonwood-willow and tamarisk–Russian olive habitat. The area can be accessed by a road that runs about three miles up the canyon, providing a number of birding spots.

Birding this area is a particular joy in springtime, when there are often waves of Western Tanagers moving through the riparian habitat, along with Lazuli Buntings, Blue Grosbeaks, and breeding-plumaged American Goldfinches. These latter birds are a treat to see in Arizona. Although they are regular winter visitors, you don't often see them in the spring in their spectacular yellow, black, and white breeding plumage. Also watch for White-throated

Swifts flying along the sides of the canyon, and for Cliff Swallows, which often build their mud nests under overhanging rocks. Some other birds seen here include Sage Thrasher, Gray Vireo, Pinyon Jay, and Cassin's Kingbird.

Perhaps the best and most consistently productive birding area is across from the store, where there is an old, abandoned campground. Riparian habitat that extends downstream from the campground has attracted a number of rare and unusual migrant and vagrant birds over the years, including Philadelphia Vireo, Brown Thrasher, Baltimore Oriole, Broad-winged Hawk, and Zone-tailed Hawk.

The Western Navajo Nation

Migrant traps and other birding areas in the western part of the reservation are even more scattered and isolated. Birders who regularly visit these spots often start out from Flagstaff and spend the day visiting two or three different locations.

North of Flagstaff, Highway 89 curves around the east side of the San Francisco Peaks and then begins a long descent toward the Little Colorado River. In the distance, you see the beautiful red, pink, and mauve rock formations of the Painted Desert. As you lose elevation from Flagstaff's 7,000 feet, the ponderosa pine trees gradually thin out and yield to pinyon-juniper habitat, home to one of my favorite resident Arizona birds, the Pinyon Jay. Along the way, you pass Sacred Mountain Trading Post (now closed) on the west side of the highway. Sacred Mountain is famous as the location where Captain America (played by Peter Fonda) stopped to gas up his motorcycle in the 1969 American movie classic *Easy Rider.*

Down the highway, Gray Mountain is little more than a spot in the road with a motel and store. However, there are a number of trees and bushes around the property. We always stop to look for birds here, knowing that even a single tree or small patch of greenery can attract birds migrating across this arid landscape. You never know when or where you will find a really interesting bird. One spring afternoon, we watched a migrating Franklin's Gull that seemed oddly out of place as it circled high over the motel.

Perhaps the best migrant trap in northeastern Arizona is at the Cameron Trading Post, which sits on the edge of the Little Colorado River gorge. The store is usually noisy and full of tourists on their way to or from the South Rim of the Grand Canyon. The lovely courtyard outside the motel, planted with flowers and bushes and shaded by cottonwood and mulberry trees, is alive with the song of water flowing in fountains. This spot has attracted a number of rare migrant and vagrant birds over the years, including species like Prothonotary Warbler, Kentucky Warbler, Magnolia Warbler, Ovenbird, American Redstart, Common Grackle, and many others. In September 2010, the state's fourth record of Great-crested Flycatcher was found here, and two Rufous-backed Robins put in an appearance in the winter of 2013.

From Cameron, birders usually travel toward Tuba City. On the way to Tuba City, you pass through the gray hills of the Chinle Formation. Teeth and jawbones of phytosaurs from the Late Triassic period are sometimes found here. In the far distance, you can see the purple outline of the San Francisco Peaks.

Just north of Tuba City on US Route 160, there is a wash

with many cottonwood trees. Known as Pasture Canyon, it's a favorite northeastern Arizona birding spot. You can park your car off the highway and follow a closed dirt road on the left for about a mile through the grove of mature trees to a reservoir. The cottonwood and Russian olive groves around the reservoir's base can be a productive place to look for migrants and vagrants in spring and fall. On the reservoir, look for migrating waterfowl, herons, grebes, ibis, and shorebirds. One spring, we found a Common Loon paddling on the water.

About a mile past the upper end of the reservoir, you come to the base of two large red sand dunes that look like something out of *Lawrence of Arabia*. This is the start of the most beautiful and scenic part of Pasture Canyon. Beyond the dunes, a small canyon with weathered sandstone walls opens up in front of you. There are several marshes in the canyon, along with some open water. In springtime, you might hear a Sora or Virginia Rail in the emergent vegetation. One spring, a migrating Northern Waterthrush was in full voice as it walked along the water's edge beneath overhanging branches. After late-summer rains, the pungent fragrance of mint bush often fills the air. The bottom of the canyon is farmed, and care should be taken not to cause any disturbance or damage to planted corn, squash, and other crops.

At times, the riparian vegetation in Pasture Canyon, as well as the scattered cottonwoods and sagebrush higher up on the canyon's sides, can be alive with migrating birds. MacGillivray's Warblers are common in migration in both the spring and fall, and seem to prefer the lush riparian vegetation, as do Common Yellowthroats. In the springtime, we almost always spot an Indigo Bunting. One spring morning, we had a small fallout of *Empido-*

nax flycatchers that seemed to be perched on just about every bush and tree. They were mostly Dusky Flycatchers, but there were also Hammond's, Cordilleran, Gray, and Willow in the mix. We spent an hour or so that morning watching and studying that amazing collection of flycatchers.

Continuing north on US Route 160 you come to Cow Springs Lake, which is situated between Tuba City and Kayenta. To reach the lake, travel 6.4 miles on US Route 160 past the Tonalea store and gas station to the spot where a large dirt road goes north (left) under a rail line. Take this road 0.6 miles to a dirt track that goes to the right at a small sandstone hill. Follow the track toward the Russian olive trees that line the lakeshore.

The lake and the extensive habitat around it are a good place to look for birds. In particular, the lake seems to attract migrating waterbirds. One spring, we observed a flock of over 90 migrating California Gulls. Unusual tern species have also shown up here, with records of Least, Caspian, and Common terns. Cow Springs Lake is also a place to look for herons—a Little Blue Heron was found here in 1989.

San Rafael Valley Grasslands

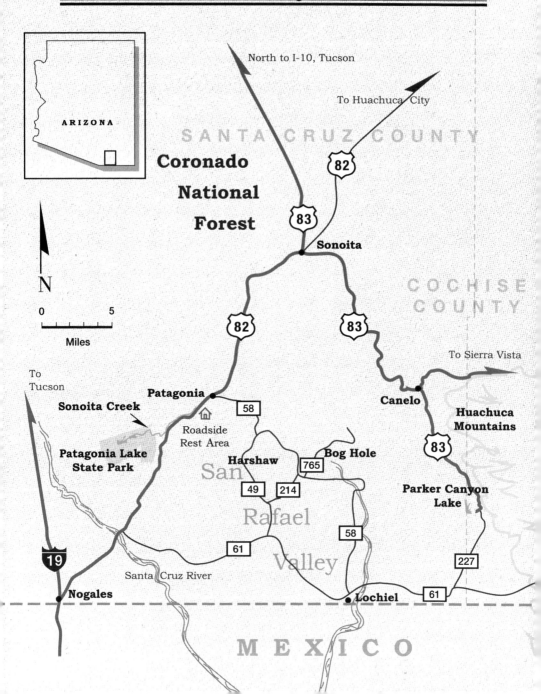

ARIZONA

N

0   5

Miles

North to I-10, Tucson

To Huachuca City

SANTA CRUZ COUNTY

Coronado

National

Forest

82

83

Sonoita

COCHISE
COUNTY

82

83

To Sierra Vista

To
Tucson

Patagonia

Sonoita Creek

Roadside
Rest Area

58

Canelo

**Huachuca
Mountains**

**Patagonia Lake
State Park**

San

Harshaw

765

Bog Hole

83

49   214

Rafael

**Parker Canyon
Lake**

58

19

61

Valley

227

Nogales

Santa Cruz River

Lochiel

61

MEXICO

Chapter 4

Visiting the San Rafael Valley Grasslands

The San Rafael Valley in southeastern Arizona is one of my favorite Arizona birding spots. The valley, which is located east of Patagonia, Arizona, is unique in having some of the state's finest remaining grassland habitat. At an elevation of about 4,000 feet, the grasslands sweep south toward the US–Mexico border. Often described as unbroken prairie grasslands, they are composed of a number of native species, including purple three-awn, sacaton, brittlegrass, and several species of grama. The San Rafael grasslands are also the headwaters of the Santa Cruz River, which flows out of the valley, crosses the international border, and then does a U-turn, flowing back across the border into Arizona.

To get there, go east from Patagonia on the road marked "San Rafael, Harshaw and Lochiel" (FR 58). At 6 miles take the left fork signed "Parker Canyon Lake". Along the way watch for Montezuma Quail in the oak woodland. At 10.5 miles you will top out on a ridge with a panoramic view of the San Rafael Valley and its grasslands.

In late summer, monsoon rains can turn the San Rafael Valley as green as Ireland. However, it is in the winter, when the nearby Canelo Hills are sometimes covered with snow, that most birders visit the area, looking for a number of specialty bird species that make the grasslands their winter home. Among those sought-after species are Short-eared Owl, Sprague's Pipit, Chestnut-collared Longspur, and Grasshopper and Baird's sparrows. You can search for these grassland species by walking through the tall grasses along the road to Bog Hole (FR 765) or parking at the power line on FR 214 and walking east.

The grasslands of the San Rafael Valley are the best place in the United States to see Baird's Sparrow in wintertime. Small numbers of these sparrows breed in eastern Montana and western South Dakota. Their US winter range, however, is limited to an area that just touches southeastern Arizona.

Baird's Sparrow can be difficult to see in the valley's thick grassland habitat. In fact, walking through the grasses in hopes of seeing one might well be described as a "fool's errand." I've attempted this on any number of occasions, repeatedly walking through the grass, flushing what I thought might be a Baird's, only to watch it fly a short distance before plunging back down and disappearing into deep grass cover.

On occasional Audubon Society field trips to the area, we tried a different approach. The group would select an area with lots of the reddish-colored grass that grows along the sides and tops of the rolling hills, and then walk out into the area and try to flush sparrows. When a likely candidate flew up and landed, the group would quickly surround it, forming a large circle. Participants slowly closed the circle by walking toward the center, hoping the bird would eventually walk or scurry into an opening or bare spot between grass clumps where we might get a look and perhaps a photograph. Even when we spotted the bird, though, it often turned out to be one of the more numerous Savannah or Vesper sparrows. This "surround" technique is commonly used by birders with difficult-to-locate species. I remember using the same method to try to find an elusive Pallas's Grasshopper Warbler in a rice field in Cambodia.

On some of our trips to the grasslands, this technique worked. On other occasions, it didn't, but it was the best strategy we could come up with; that is, until someone figured out that the easiest way to see Baird's Sparrow in the San Rafael Valley is to start birding right at sunrise and drive the main road (FR 58) through the valley—particularly the first three or four miles after the ridge—watching for Baird's perched on the wires of the barbed-wire fences that parallel the road. It seems that sparrows, including Baird's, like to perch on the fence wires, perhaps trying to warm up or dry off after a night in wet grasses. Even at that, you still have to look through a lot of Savannah and Vesper sparrows and an occasional Grasshopper Sparrow before you spot a Baird's.

Since much of the valley is private land and off-limits to birders, including the Vaca Ranch Corrals at 2.2 miles from the ridge, it is advisable to do most of your birding along FR 58 watching for birds perched on fences and trees. It is also very helpful to know the songs and calls of the birds you want to find.

The Grasshopper Sparrows in the valley are called Arizona Grasshopper Sparrows. This race or subspecies is found in southeastern Arizona, extreme southwestern New Mexico, and parts of northern Sonora, Mexico. They are resident breeders. Their insect-like song can often be heard right after the onset of summer monsoon rains.

Another famous winter resident of the San Rafael Valley is Sprague's Pipit. The first time I ever saw one of these birds was in late February. What struck me most about it were its legs, which were a bright, bubble gum–pink color. Other than the legs, Sprague's Pipit is a nondescript, plain-looking bird, even for a pipit.

Its dark, button-like eyes stand out on what is often described as a blank-looking face. It was named by John James Audubon for Isaac Sprague, an artist who accompanied Audubon on a trip up the Missouri River.

Like Baird's Sparrow, Sprague's Pipit can be difficult to find in the San Rafael Valley. They occur in relatively small numbers and don't perch on fences, so finding them can be a real challenge. In fact, more often than not, birders just seem to happen upon the bird walking along the side of the road or standing in a bare patch in the grass. These pipits seem to prefer more open areas with shorter grasses.

Often, the best way to find Sprague's Pipit is to walk through the grasses off FR 765 or FR 214. On occasion, you can flush one. When they do flush, they're easy to identify, often giving a loud and distinctive "squeent" call as they fly up and away. They also seem to fly higher than sparrows do before plunging back into the grass.

As you walk through areas with dense, tall grass, you might also flush a wintering Short-eared Owl. The San Rafael Valley is one of the best places in the state to see these wintering owls. Their numbers can vary from year to year depending upon the rodent prey base. You can sometimes see them right from the main road hunting over the grasslands just at sunrise or at dusk. On occasion, you can also spot them perched alongside roads after dark.

Sometimes when I'm birding the San Rafael Valley, I get bored looking for grassland species and need a diversion. So what do I do? Well, I take some time off to look at ravens' noses. What!

Ravens are fairly common in the San Rafael Valley. I often spot them hopping about at corrals or stock tanks or perched in tall cottonwoods that grow in the valley's drainages. Most are Common Ravens, but when I see one, I always wonder if it might in fact be a Chihuahuan Raven. The ranges of these two almost identical–looking birds overlap in much of southeastern Arizona. The heart of the Arizona breeding range of the Chihuahuan Raven is slightly to the east of the San Rafael Valley toward Sierra Vista, and in areas farther west of Sierra Vista, as well. However, both species do occur in the San Rafael Valley, so I am always left wondering which one I'm looking at. Trips to the valley can afford a unique opportunity to take up that most challenging of Arizona bird identification problems: trying to separate Common and Chihuahuan ravens.

The Chihuahuan Raven is slightly smaller than the Common, but this is of no help unless you happen to get lucky and see the two species together. Likewise, it is said that the calls of the two species are different, but I've never had much luck with this, either, even when I do happen to hear one calling. What has been touted as the best way to differentiate the two species is to look at the color of the feather bases on the birds' neck. In the Common, the feather bases are a grayish color, while in the Chihuahuan, they are white. These bases, however, can only be seen when there is a strong wind that can, so to speak, "ruffle the bird's feathers." But what about on one of those frequent, non-windy days?

Well, that's why I like to practice looking at ravens' noses. When I get bored, I haul out my spotting scope and begin analyzing them. Actually, I try to look at the bird's nasal bristles (the long, hair-like feathers that cover the nostrils). In Common Ravens, the nasal bristles are fairly short, with more of the bill showing, giving the impression of a longer, thicker beak. With the Chihuahuan Raven, on the other hand, the nasal bristles are longer, extending out toward the end of the bill, making it look shorter. If all this sounds a bit too esoteric, and you just want to see a Chihuahuan Raven, you can probably assume that the flock of ravens you see in wintertime in Sierra Vista are Chihuahuans.

A rather common bird, and one that is easy to find in the San Rafael Valley, is the Lilian's Meadowlark, a subspecies of Eastern Meadowlark that may in fact be a separate species. They often perch on fence wires or flush as you walk through the taller grasses. The valley is an ideal place to study these birds, and more importantly, to learn their distinctive song and buzzy call note. The ranges of Lilian's and Western meadowlarks overlap, especially in northern and eastern Arizona. It is always difficult separating them visually, so voice identification is one of the easiest and surest ways to do it. Even in wintertime, you can often hear the Lilian's song, which is several whistled notes, very unlike the complex warbling song of Western. The Lilian's call is an electric, buzzy-sounding "zeet." It reminds me of the flight call of the Dickcissel.

Longspurs are another sought-after winter visitor to the San Rafael Valley. Most are Chestnut-collared, with occasional McCown's and, very rarely, Lapland. Chestnut-collared Longspurs often flush from the grasses or occasionally fly in to drink at stock tanks along FR 58. In flight, they give characteristic and easy-to-identify "kiddle kiddle" call notes. They sometimes perch on fence wires. In late winter, you can sometimes see males that are molting into spring plumage—these show black smudges on the lower breast and belly. Once in a while, you can spot a McCown's Longspur. They are hard to pick out in flight, but when they're on the ground, you can usually spot them by their larger, more conical bills.

Chapter 4

The valley's grasslands are also a great place to look for wintering raptors. Watch for Ferruginous Hawk, Northern Harrier, and an occasional Golden Eagle. The area is also one of the better places in the state to find White-tailed Kite and wintering Merlin. The grasslands are occasionally visited in winter by Northern Rough-legged Hawks. Southeastern Arizona is just about as far south as these Arctic breeders get in the United States. You can occasionally spot one flying low over the grasslands or hovering nearly motionless in the wind, looking for rodent prey.

Tucson and Phoenix Audubon Societies often have field trips to the San Rafael Valley in winter. Whether with a group or on your own a visit to the grasslands is an unforgettable experience.

Chapter 5: Fun Ways To Count Birds

Most birders are listers: i.e., they keep formal records of the bird species they see and identify. Birders often keep county, state, national, and even international lists, as well as a life list. In this chapter, you'll learn about many other ways you can have fun counting birds, including big days, big years, and citizen science oriented activities like Christmas Bird Counts, Breeding Bird Surveys, hawk watches, and winter waterfowl surveys. "A Big Day in the Chiricahuas" takes you on a 24-hour "big day" through the Chiricahua Mountains. "Citizen Science and Field Trips" gets you started as a citizen scientist. Then join me as I set out to find all 13 Arizona owl species in "A Big Year for Owls."

A Big Day in the Chiricahuas

Few birding experiences are more challenging and exciting than a "big day." The object of a big day is to find as many different bird species as possible in a 24-hour period. The American Birding Association formulates official big day rules and keeps and publishes big day records for most states and Canadian provinces. The current Arizona record is 199 species found by a big day team in southeastern Arizona in August of 1998.

A variation on a big day is the "birdathon," which raises money for local Audubon Society chapters by getting people to pledge money for each bird species found by a birdathon team in a 24-hour period. Whether a big day or birdathon or some combination of the two, these events can test and hone your birding skills like nothing else. They're also a lot of fun.

Routes for these events are carefully planned and designed to cover as many habitats and birding "hot spots" as possible in order to maximize the number of species seen, with the goal of raising money or even breaking an official big day state record. No doubt there is a highly competitive element to them. In fact, on some of our big day trips, we jokingly told members of other teams that nothing short of a dire emergency would get us to deviate from our schedule and chosen route.

Perhaps no place lends itself to a big day better than the Chiricahua Mountains in southeastern Arizona. A narrow dirt road winds and twists up the mountain over Onion Saddle, connecting Chiricahua National Monument on the west side with the small community of Portal on the east side. Driving this road, you pass through a variety of different habitats in an area many people consider the finest bird-watching location in the United States.

I fondly remember several of these trips done with friends in the 1990s. We usually started our big day at the campground at Chiricahua National Monument, rolling out of sleeping bags at midnight after a few fitful hours of sleep out on the hard ground. We always wondered what bird would be the first big day species of the trip. One would logically think it would be some kind of night bird, like an owl or nightjar. That, however, was not always the case. On one occasion, the first bird was an insomniac Canyon Wren, giving its beautiful descending song in the darkness. On another, it was a Western Kingbird, calling from a perch in a tree somewhere off in the distance. Actually, the kingbird should not have been a surprise. In Mexico, kingbirds are often called *madrugadores*, or "early risers."

The reason for getting up in the dead of night was to look for owls, nighthawks, and nightjars. These trips produced good numbers of owls—sometimes seven or eight different species. Shortly after midnight, we usually heard Elf Owls calling in the large sycamore trees along nearby Bonita Creek. These small owls are actually the most common of Arizona's 13 different owl species, and are also one of the smallest owls in the world. Western Screech-Owls could usually be coaxed into view somewhere in the camp-ground, and if we were lucky, we would hear the raspy, hissing call of a Barn Owl as it flew over the adjacent grasslands. The real thrill, however, was searching up the road toward Massai Point for Mexican Spotted Owls, which nested in the area for a number of years. On several big day trips, we had the good fortune of hearing their hair-raising calls from cliffs high up on the Arizona cypress–clad slopes above us.

As the night progressed, we would slowly drive up the road through the darkness toward Onion Saddle. Along the way, we always heard Whiskered Screech-Owls giving their Morse code-like calls. As we drove higher into the pine belt, we would begin to hear Flammulated Owl, a small neotropical owl species that it seems you can always hear but virtually never see.

The nighttime sky was often spectacular, with stars that seemed to jump out at us. The Chiricahua Mountains are, in fact, a well known dark-sky site. One year (1997) we had incredible views of comet Hale-Bopp streaming through the night sky toward the western horizon. In early May, it was usually cold in the

Chiricahuas, with temperatures hovering in the low 40s. We knew, however, that by the time we reached Patagonia later in the day, the temperature would be pushing 90 degrees.

We usually arrived near Onion Saddle just as dawn was breaking. This is the time we often heard a Northern Pygmy-Owl calling in the distance. We would also listen for Northern Saw-whet Owl. One year, we heard a Saw-whet nearby and were able to locate its perch in the lower branches of a Douglas-fir tree. The bird was so tame we could almost reach out and touch it.

By 6 o'clock, we were on top of the mountains headed for Rustler Park, looking for its many and varied montane species to add to our list. It's amazing to consider that these tall Engelmann spruce and Douglas-fir trees, reminiscent of some dark boreal forest in Canada, sit atop mountains which are just a few miles from the US–Mexico border. Many of the birds we saw there were boreal species. In the spruce and fir trees surrounding Rustler Park, we would look for species like Golden-crowned Kinglet, Evening Grosbeak, Red Crossbill, Pine Siskin, and Northern Goshawk. Beautiful and distinctive songsters like Hermit Thrush and American Robin could always be heard in the area. We also counted on finding Chiricahua specialties like Eastern Bluebird, Mexican Chickadee, Olive and Red-faced warblers, and Hepatic Tanager.

Driving down from Onion Saddle early in the morning toward Cave Creek Campground, we kept an eye out along the road for Montezuma Quail, which we sometimes saw crouched down as we passed. We were often moving at a fairly good clip, going too fast to stop and watch these remarkably patterned birds. Big day trips demand that you keep moving from one birding spot to another. That fact would create a certain tension. On the one hand, there was temptation to spend extra time looking for a specific species you knew must be around, and on the other, the need to keep to the schedule and timetable.

Sticking close to our schedule, we would arrive at Cave Creek Campground around half past six. Here, we had a chance to add a whole new group of birds to our growing list. This location offers numerous "must find" species, birds we would not have a chance of seeing or hearing somewhere else along the route. (Yes, big day rules do allow you to count "heard-only" species.)

A hike up Cave Creek Canyon along the streamside trail usually produced such famous residents as Sulphur-bellied Flycatcher, Dusky-capped Flycatcher, Greater Pewee, Arizona Woodpecker, Mexican Jay, Blue-throated Hummingbird, Painted Redstart, and of course, the Elegant Trogon, whose turkey-like, croaking call we usually heard off in the distance at just about the time we had given up hope of finding it. On one trip, we encountered a black-tailed rattlesnake warming itself on a flat rock as we walked back down the trail.

Small side trips near Portal took us to rocky canyon slopes (where we would try to tally Black-chinned Sparrow) and to Willow Tank, on the road to Rodeo. Willow Tank is a small, watery oasis filled with clear pumped groundwater and surrounded by willows, cattails, and mesquite. Sometimes, we got lucky and found small fallouts of warblers and other passerines in the mesquite, and once, we had a flock of Willets. These unexpected shorebirds were still dressed in drab non-breeding plumage, but they showed their striking black-and-white wing pattern when they flew.

Birding Arizona

After leaving the Chiricahua Mountains, our next stop was Willcox, Arizona. Willcox is in many ways the quintessential small, dusty western town, with a few stores, a Dairy Queen, and some rusty windmills scattered about. Train tracks bisect the town. It is best known as the hometown of Rex Allen, a famous cowboy singer and actor of the 1950s and 1960s. We usually arrived in Willcox around noon, just in time to break out the peanut butter and jelly sandwiches. Easy to make and eat on the move, peanut butter and jelly sandwiches were a big day staple.

If you're going to have a really big, big day, you can't do it without solid representation from among the shorebird family. Near Willcox, Lake Cochise and the adjacent playa can be a magnet for shorebirds in springtime, depending on water conditions. Ideally, there should be neither too little nor too much water, but lots of exposed mudflats and islands. Water conditions, however, can vary substantially from year to year.

It was always with a fair amount of anticipation that we would pull into the Lake Cochise parking area, expecting to see species like Western, Least, and Spotted sandpipers, as well as Greater Yellowlegs, Long-billed Dowitcher, Black-necked Stilt, American Avocet, and Wilson's Phalarope. We sometimes picked up a migrating gull species like Ring-billed or Franklin's, and there were always a few lingering ducks. If conditions were good and the timing was right, we might add more unusual shorebird species to our list; maybe a Dunlin, Red-necked Phalarope, or Semipalmated Plover. And then there was always the possibility of something really rare, like White-rumped Sandpiper or Hudsonian Godwit, two species that are known to drop into Willcox in the spring once every few years or so.

Chapter 5

From Willcox, it was a nonstop drive to the Patagonia area, host to a number of famous birding spots, including the Patagonia-Sonoita Creek Preserve, the Patagonia Roadside Rest Area, Kino Springs, and the hummingbird feeders at the Patons' house (now Tucson Audubon's Paton Center for Hummingbirds). Along the way, we closely watched roadside fences, hoping to spot a Grasshopper Sparrow, Eastern Meadowlark, or even Lark Bunting, which at this time of year is spectacular in its black-and-white breeding plumage.

Arriving in the Patagonia area in midafternoon, we would stop at Patons and then do a quick hike through the preserve, where we usually found Violet-crowned Hummingbird, Gray Hawk, Northern Beardless-Tyrannulet, Lazuli Bunting, Vermilion Flycatcher, and other species. A stop at the roadside rest area would sometimes, but not always, produce one of my favorite southeastern Arizona birds, the Thick-billed Kingbird. More often than not, the kingbird was located by its loud, head-turning call. Some years, we wouldn't find it: maybe it simply had not yet arrived to nest. Our big days were usually too early in the year for another famous summer resident, the Rose-throated Becard. But the rest area was always a reliable spot for Rufous-crowned Sparrow, White-throated Swift, and Rock Wren.

Just up the road at Kino Springs, we could almost always count on getting Common Ground-Dove, Pyrrhuloxia, and perhaps a few duck species we had missed at Willcox, including one of my favorites, the Black-bellied Whistling-Duck. We would spend some time looking for Inca Dove and Abert's Towhee, both fairly common species in southern Arizona, but difficult to find on our chosen route.

Birding Arizona

Our last stop was always Nogales, Arizona. We would end the big day in a marshy area near the Nogales Country Club, looking for Black-crowned Night-Heron and Green Heron while listening for Virginia Rail. More often than not, we would hear the Virginia Rail's "kidick kidick kidick" call just at dusk. When it was too dark to continue, we would begin the long drive back to Phoenix. That first big day bird, heard as we'd rolled up our sleeping bags just after midnight in the Chiricahuas the night before, now seemed like a distant memory. Although the rules permitted us to continue counting birds up to midnight, the idea of chasing a few more species in the darkness was usually more than our bone-weary bodies could take.

We never broke the big day state record, but one year, we managed a very respectable 184 species on this route.

Footnote: The Horseshoe II fire in 2011 burned large areas in the Chiricahua Mountains. Rustler Park was severely burned, with loss of much of the spruce-fir habitat around the park. On a recent trip to the area, the birding was still excellent, with the usual Chiricahua specialty birds being easy to find. In many fire-burned areas, aspen trees are regenerating. Hopefully, in the coming years, this area will grow back to some of its previous beauty.

Citizen Science and Field Trips

Besides big days, there are lots of other ways for birders to have fun. One of the most enjoyable and satisfying of these is to participate in or lead **birding field trips**. Field trips are a fun way not only to learn to identify birds, but to learn new birding locations and get to know fellow birders. They are especially valuable for beginning birders. When I was a novice birder, I was fortunate to go on many field trips to interesting birding spots with the Maricopa and Tucson Audubon Societies. That's how I found out the location of good fall shorebirding spots in and around Phoenix, where to look for Black Vultures and Crested Caracaras near Sells, Arizona, and where to look for Mississippi Kites along the San Pedro River.

Arizona birders have many field trip options from which to choose. Local Audubon Societies all have regularly scheduled trips to many parts of Arizona. You can find a field trip just about any day of the week, any month of the year. In addition, botanical gardens and museums often regularly conduct bird walks. Two of my favorites guided bird walks are those at the Boyce Thompson Arboretum near Superior and the Desert Botanical Garden in Phoenix.

Boyce Thompson Arboretum is a great Arizona birding location. You can bird there on your own or take one of their frequent bird walks, which are led by experienced and knowledgeable leaders. The arboretum's many plants and trees attract a variety of nesting and wintering bird species. In spring and fall, the area teems with migrating birds. The list of rare and unusual species seen at the arboretum is long and includes Tufted Flycatcher, Rufous-backed Robin, Varied Thrush, and Yellow-throated Vireo. Every spring and fall, the arboretum celebrates the arrival and departure of resident Turkey Vultures. During the summer months, the vultures can often be observed roosting in the area's tall eucalyptus trees.

The Desert Botanical Garden has weekly guided bird walks.

Birding Arizona

It's a wonderful place to see many of our more familiar Sonoran Desert breeding species, including that quintessential western bird, the Greater Roadrunner. In central Phoenix, the Arizona Audubon Society Center hosts weekly bird walks along the Salt River.

As you gain experience, it's fun to lead birding field trips. Being a volunteer leader is a great way to improve your birding skills. It also requires multitasking. Having to manage a group, locate birds, and try to get them in the spotting scope for participants to see can be a real challenge. One of my most enjoyable birding experiences has been leading an annual field trip for the Maricopa Audubon Society to the lakes around Flagstaff to see wintering passerines and raptors, and especially, migrating waterfowl. It reminds me, however, that being a field trip leader can sometimes be a very humbling experience. During a driving snowstorm on one mid-March trip, I spotted what I thought was an eagle perched in a far-off tree. The eagle turned out to be a perched Mourning Dove.

Many of the fun things you can do as a birder involve citizen science. Citizen scientists are nonprofessionals who go out and gather and collect data for professionals to analyze and use. According to Professor David Pearson at Arizona State University, many areas of traditional research biology have now been "largely turned over to amateurs."

For birders, being a citizen scientist usually means counting birds. These activities are not only fun, but they contribute valuable information about bird population trends. The information collected helps inform and guide conservation organizations and land managers in monitoring and protecting bird species. Today, for example, thousands of volunteer participants input their bird sightings into **Cornell Lab of Ornithology's eBird website**, which is creating one of the most ambitious biodiversity databanks in existence. Each February, the Cornell Lab and National Audubon Society sponsor another important data-collecting event, the annual **Great Backyard Bird Count**. Birders are asked to count and record birds seen in their backyard for as little as 15 minutes (or as long as they wish) on one or more days of the four-day event and report their sightings online. This information provides an important snapshot of wintering bird population trends and fluctuations.

Perhaps the most famous of these citizen-science efforts is the National Audubon Society's annual **Christmas Bird Count**. First established in 1900, these counts are now the world's longest-running uninterrupted bird census. In 2016, over 73,000 participants counted birds in about 2,500 "count circles," each one 15 miles in diameter. Count participants are assigned areas in the count circles and spend the day in the field, counting the number of birds they observe. After the count, they often meet and tally the results at compilation dinners, a lively social event where you meet with fellow birders and talk about that rare bird you did (or did not!) find.

In Arizona, there are over 35 different Christmas counts each year during the latter part of December and in early January. You can find a count in which to participate just about anyplace in the state, including tribal lands. For many years, the Maricopa Audubon Society and the Gila Salt River Indian Community have conducted an annual winter bird count on Salt River tribal lands south of Phoenix. Tribal members, including children, travel with Audubon members to parts of the reservation normally closed to visitors. After the bird count, the tribe provides participants with lunch and a cultural presentation, which can include songs, poetry, and dances about birds.

Another fun way to hone your birding skills and participate in citizen science is to run a **Breeding Bird Survey route**. These surveys are sponsored by the US Geological Survey's Patuxent Wildlife Research Center. Volunteers are asked to select and then run a 25-mile survey route each spring. Each route is divided into half-mile stops. Volunteers are asked to spend three minutes at each of the 50 stops and record all birds seen and, even more importantly, all birds heard. These surveys are an excellent way to learn birdsongs, as many of the counted birds are only heard, not seen. Data from these surveys have been used to determine population trends for more than 400 bird species and to mark the decline of many neotropical species and about 55 percent of grassland bird species.

For several years, I ran a Breeding Bird Survey route south of Mormon Lake in northern Arizona. One summer morning, a beautiful male Northern Goshawk flew out onto the shoulder of the roadway where I had stopped to count. That was one of the many rewards of having to get up at half past three in the morning to start my route.

The Arizona Field Ornithologists have a number of very interesting **bird survey projects** in which birders can participate. They offer regular field trips or field expeditions to various parts of the state. One goal of these is expanding our knowledge of Arizona bird distribution. Among the many trips they have sponsored are those to the White Mountains to survey for Canada Jay and look for possible breeding Wilson's Warbler, and to western Arizona to survey for wintering Gray Vireo. They often plan these field expeditions to little-known or under-birded areas. In the winter, the Arizona Field Ornithologists sponsor a raptor survey at the Santa Cruz Flats, located along the basin of the Santa Cruz River, which flows northwest across the county toward the Gila River. In recent years, this area has become one of the most reliable places in Arizona to see Crested Caracara. The Arizona Field Ornithologists also help coordinate the Global Big Day, an important worldwide bird migration count sponsored by the Cornell Lab of Ornithology and eBird.

The Arizona Game and Fish Department sponsors a different survey, this one of waterfowl. Phoenix-area residents and visitors can spend a delightful day in mid-January, using only a modest amount of physical effort as they scan for waterfowl on urban lakes and golf course ponds. This survey provides valuable information about the seasonal status of wintering geese, ducks, herons, grebes, and shorebirds. It has documented the presence of between 40,000 and 50,000 waterbirds of 50 to 60 species in winter. According to Troy Corman, a bird expert with the Arizona Game and Fish Department, this annual survey has shown that man-made urban water bodies account for the highest density and diversity of wintering waterbirds of any place of equal size in Arizona.

For Arizona birders who like to watch and count migrating raptors, there are a number of **hawk-watching** opportunities. In recent years, there have been informal hawk watches along the Santa Cruz and San Pedro rivers that count northerly-migrating hawks—especially Common Black-Hawk—that use these rivers as migration corridors in springtime. There are also fall raptor watches at the South Rim of the Grand Canyon at both Yaki and Lipan points.

Birding Arizona

For more adventurous birders, there are many new areas to explore that could potentially be places to watch and count raptors; places, for example, like the summits of Mount Ord or the Pinal Mountains, both in central Arizona.

Besides participating in citizen science projects, birders can use their skills to raise money for worthwhile environmental causes. In addition to **big days** and **birdathons**, there are other ways birders can raise money. One of the more unique of these is the "**big sit**." Participants stay in one spot and spend several hours sitting and counting birds that fly into their count area. People are asked in advance to donate or make pledges based on the number of birds observed.

Listing birds is not only fun, but it can be useful, as well. When I first started keeping a list, I wrote down each new species next to the drawing of the bird in my field-worn *Peterson Field Guide*. With the eBird program, keeping bird lists has become easier and more automated. For many years, I've kept a yearly Arizona list. Looking at lists from past years shows me which birds I haven't seen in a while, so I can make an effort to get out and see them again. On average, I see about 270 to 300 different bird species in Arizona every year. This usually requires several visits to a variety of different habitat types.

In addition to listing, there are many other fun and unique ways to challenge yourself and hone your birding skills. In the following section, you'll hear the story of the year I decided to set out and find all 13 Arizona owl species in one year. You could just as easily have your own big year; for example, by trying to find all the Arizona-breeding flycatchers, or making this your year to find all of

Arizona's ducks, hawks, or shorebirds. Whatever a "big year" means to you, happy birding!

A Big Year for Owls

There is no better way to start off the New Year than to walk out the front door in the pre-dawn darkness and hear two different owl species calling.

That's what happened to me on January 1, 2009, at my home in Phoenix. In the distance, I heard the faint, bouncing ball–like call of a Western Screech-Owl, a small owl occasionally found in urban areas around the city. From the opposite direction came the low, hooting call of a Great Horned Owl, a fairly common resident of our neighborhood. I sometimes hear the pair, but rarely hear both at the same time, as happened that morning.

With my annual Arizona bird list off to a good start—at least with the owls—I decided it might be fun to try to find all 13 of the state's owl species in one year. Arizona has more owl species than just about any other state. While it's not uncommon to find as many as seven or eight species on a big day in springtime, getting all 13 in one year would be a significant challenge. Finding them would be an adventure, with lots of daytime and nighttime treks into many different habitats in many different parts of the state.

Some owl species would be harder to find than others. Three in particular—the Ferruginous Pygmy-Owl, Long-eared Owl, and Short-eared Owl—would be difficult for varying reasons. The Ferruginous Pygmy-Owl is an endangered species whose numbers continue to decrease due to habitat loss. Populations of

Birding Arizona

Long-eared Owl, a widespread but erratic breeder, and Short-eared Owl, a winter visitor, often fluctuate depending on the abundance of prey. It would take persistence and a little luck to find them all.

In early February, I decided to try for owl number three. Northern Saw-whet Owl, a small nocturnal owl, begins calling in the high country in late winter, but populations tend to be sporadic in distribution, and sightings are scattered across the state. I opted to search on the San Francisco Peaks near Flagstaff—the highest mountain in the state, and an area where the bird breeds. The snow was deep and the temperatures in the low 20s as I slowly drove up the Snowbowl Road toward Agassiz Peak. In the sky, Venus was shining in the west while Orion wielded his sword high above my head.

At my third stop, a Northern Saw-whet Owl was calling off in the distance. I followed the monotonous tooting through the snow and, with the aid of a flashlight, I was able to see the bird perched on the limb of a 60-foot Douglas-fir. Shivering in the cold, I felt fortunate that I would not have to search for Snowy Owl. Yes, there is a 1970 Arizona sight record of three Snowy Owls flying through a winter storm. Thankfully, at least for my big year purposes, the Snowy Owl remains on the state's hypothetical list.

My fourth and fifth owl species came just two weeks later. In late February, I was birding a large irrigation pond south of Phoenix, looking not for owls but for wintering ducks. To my surprise, a Barn Owl burst out of dense tamarisk growing along the water's edge. For a moment or two, the cold west wind seemed to hold it suspended in the air as it beat its wings before flying up and away. Not expecting to find it so easily, I was glad to check it off early in my quest.

Later that day, near Gila Bend, a small town southwest of the city, I spotted a Burrowing Owl, a small diurnal owl, standing on a canal bank next to a flooded alfalfa field. This species is often seen in agricultural areas west of Phoenix. Its erect posture and wide-eyed look always remind me of J. R. R. Tolkien's hobbits.

In mid-April, a friend and I drove to Organ Pipe Cactus National Monument in south-central Arizona in search of the rarest of my target owls, the Ferruginous Pygmy-Owl. The monument is one of a handful of sites in the state where the species is hanging on after decades of decline. The property, which is run by the National Park Service, preserves the rugged upper and lower Sonoran Desert habitat the bird requires.

The springtime desert landscape was spectacular that morning. Fiery red ocotillo and stately organ pipe cactus were scattered among bright yellow palo verde trees. Around seven o'clock, we heard one of these elusive owls calling from thick vegetation along a rocky wash. We were ecstatic and also very lucky. Surveyors in Arizona have located only about 20 Ferruginous Pygmy-Owls each year since 2003. The owl continued to call incessantly for the next 20 minutes. After much effort, we finally found it perched about four feet off the ground in a creosote bush. Eventually, a small army of songbirds led by four or five scolding Black-tailed Gnatcatchers and two or three brave Verdins mobbed it and chased it away.

The mountains of southeastern Arizona are a great place to look for owls. One of the most sought-after species is the Spotted Owl, a large, rather tame bird typically found in narrow, shady canyons in isolated ranges like the Chiricahuas, Huachucas, and

Birding Arizona

Santa Ritas. Arizona's birds are Mexican Spotted Owls, a threatened subspecies that occurs from Utah and Colorado south to western Texas and the Sierra Madre in Mexico.

In early May came reports of a Spotted Owl that was being seen regularly in Miller Canyon in the Huachuca Mountains. My wife, Eleanor, and I decided to look for it one Sunday morning. As we walked upstream along Miller Creek, Red-faced Warblers, Painted Redstarts, and Dusky-capped Flycatchers seemed to be singing from every tree. Suddenly, Eleanor, who was walking about 30 feet behind me, called out, "I have the owl."

I turned around and was surprised to see it perched on a limb over the trail. It was hidden in the bright green leaves of a bigtooth maple tree, and I had walked right underneath. We spent the next half-hour watching it. From time to time, it would open its dark eyes, flex one of its claws, and carefully preen its beautiful spotted breast feathers. We left owl number seven exactly where we found him.

Two weeks later, I drove to Ganado, a small community in the heart of the vast Navajo tribal lands in northeastern Arizona. Struggling through a dense Russian olive thicket in Ganado Wash looking for spring migrants and raptors, I decided to look at a large nest nearby. Common Ravens and a Great Horned Owl had successively occupied it over the previous two years.

Reaching the site, I saw a large bird partially hidden behind tree branches near the nest. I assumed it was the Great Horned Owl, but on second look, it was obviously much slimmer than a Great Horned. It had a narrow face with vertical stripes and two prominent ear tufts. It was owl number eight, a Long-eared Owl! To add to the thrill, a fluffy, newly fledged juvenile (often referred to as a "brancher") was perched nearby.

The Long-eared occurs across Mexico, the United States, and Canada, but in Arizona it's not reliable anywhere. Nomadic and shy, it is one of the least-known owls of Arizona. Less than five months into my quest, I'd found it. Even better, there were now only five owls to go.

What a difference four months can make! Returning to the San Francisco Peaks in mid-June, I found meadows covered in blooming Rocky Mountain iris instead of snow and ice.

My quarry was the small Flammulated Owl, a neotropical species that inhabits western pine and fir forests from British Columbia to central Mexico in the summer. I had no trouble locating it. In fact, three Flammulated Owls were hooting softly in a three-mile stretch of mountain road about an hour after dark. In three or four months, most of these owls would be gone, making the long flight to their wintering grounds in southern Mexico and Central America.

A week later, I went in search of another high-elevation species, the Northern Pygmy-Owl, after receiving a report that two had been heard on Mount Ord, northeast of Phoenix.

Identifying owls by sound is sometimes not as easy as it might seem, especially at night. Many distant sounds can be mistaken for owl calls, including barking dogs, scraping tree branches, or creaky windmills. One windy spring night high in the Chiricahua Mountains, my friends and I were fooled into thinking we heard a Northern Saw-whet Owl. The call turned out to be the distant backup alarm of a front-end loader.

Birding Arizona

Thankfully, the Northern Pygmy-Owl on Mount Ord was most obliging, responding unmistakably to whistled imitations of its call. It was now 10 down and three to go.

Perhaps no place is more fun to look for owls than Madera Canyon in the Santa Rita Mountains. In fact, on cool summer evenings, it is almost an event. The canyon's woodland is home to a number of cooperative owl species, including both Whiskered and Western screech-owls, Elf Owl, Great Horned Owl, and, less commonly, Northern Pygmy-Owl, Flammulated Owl, and Spotted Owl. However, looking for owls in Madera Canyon can be tricky; sometimes, you're not sure if you are listening to an owl or to another birder playing a recording in the darkness. A missed cue on an iPod or tape recorder might have you thinking a Boreal Owl is somewhere off in the oaks.

In early August, I spent an evening in Madera Canyon looking for Whiskered Screech-Owl and Elf Owl. The Whiskered Screech-Owl is a small, nonmigratory, high-elevation bird found from southeastern Arizona and southwestern New Mexico south to Nicaragua. The Elf Owl, the world's smallest owl, breeds in Arizona, New Mexico, Texas, and northern Mexico and winters in the Sierra Madre region of western Mexico. It has been described as "the most abundant owl in Arizona."

Above the campground, distant flashes of lightning from the gathering monsoon occasionally illuminated the granite peaks of the Santa Ritas. As darkness deepened, I could hear the song of the Mexican Whip-poor-will as it flew through the night, scooping up insects.

A little later, two Western Screech-Owls began a duet,

Chapter 5

calling back and forth, and shortly after, a Whiskered Screech-Owl chimed in with its Morse code–like call. The Whiskered eventually flew in and perched in an alligator juniper. It stared at me with its bright yellow eyes. At about 10 o'clock, an Elf Owl began calling in the large sycamores along Madera Creek, its yipping call competing with the loud voices of canyon treefrogs.

There was one more owl to find, but my search for the Short-eared Owl would have to wait until fall. The species, which winters across most of the United States and northern Mexico, is rare in Arizona, and is recorded only from October to March. I hadn't seen one in the state since 1985.

In spite of repeated attempts, including several searches in agricultural areas southwest of Phoenix, I couldn't find the bird. In late December, I made a final try, this time in the San Rafael Valley south of Patagonia. The valley's lush grasslands are famous for such wintering specialties as Sprague's Pipit, Baird's Sparrow, and Chestnut-collared and McCown's longspurs. The grasslands are also one of the more reliable locations for Short-eared Owls.

My search for the owl began at dusk as a full moon—a decade-ending blue moon—rose over the Canelo Hills. Driving slowly along dusty roads, I paid special attention to Border Patrol vehicles; at one point, the officers were more than a little curious about my activities.

I soon spotted an owl in the road ahead. It was the right size for Short-eared, but it flew off before I could grab my binoculars. A little farther along, another owl was sitting at the roadside. This time, there was no doubt: it was a streaked, buffy Short-eared Owl. It turned and glared at me, its yellow-orange eyes blazing in the lights.

That blue-moon owl was a perfect ending to my yearlong quest. I don't know how many people have found all the Arizona owl species in one year or have even tried. For me, however, the experience was unforgettable. I visited almost every part of the state, from snowcapped mountains in the north to deserts and grasslands in the south. I will always remember the Ferruginous Pygmy-Owl staring at me out of the creosote bush, and the Mexican Spotted Owl calmly watching Eleanor and me from its perch in the maple tree. What a year!

Chapter 6: Birding and the Environment

Birding leads almost inevitably to a deeper understanding of, and appreciation for, the complexity and beauty of the natural world around us. In "Things Birds Do for Us," you'll discover the many ways we benefit from the activity of birds. "Habitat Matters" discusses the importance of preserving and protecting the riparian, forest, and grassland habitats that are home to Arizona's many bird species. "Reintroduced Species: A Cautionary Tale" examines lessons to be learned from attempts to reintroduce three extirpated species: Thick-billed Parrot, Masked Bobwhite, and California Condor.

Things Birds Do for Us

We like birds for many reasons: their beautiful songs, brightly colored plumage, and most of all, their ability to fly through the air. Birds have always fascinated us. We write books about them, paint them, and celebrate them in poetry. From the earliest of times, humans have used birds for religious purposes and even worshiped them. In the Southwest, the remains of Thick-billed Parrots and Scarlet Macaws have been found ceremonially buried at a number of archaeological sites, including Tuzigoot and Wupatki national monuments in Arizona.

Birds provide us with food for our tables, fertilizer for our crops, feathers for our pillows, and down for our jackets. We keep them as pets, use them for sport, and train them to carry messages. Japanese and Chinese fishermen use cormorants to help them catch fish. Some speculate that in the future, we may be able to use the exceptional memory and face-recognition ability of Common Ravens and American Crows to help find people who are lost.

There are many ways we benefit, either directly or indirectly, from the activity of birds. Take a look around and you'll see birds controlling insect and rodent populations, pollinating plants and flowers, replanting trees in forests, cleaning up and sanitizing our surroundings, and acting as barometers of environmental health.

One of the most important services birds perform is controlling insect populations. Insects provide the bulk of the diet of many birds. This fact is reflected in the names of bird families like "flycatchers" and "gnatcatchers." Grasshoppers comprise much of the diet of American Kestrels, and caterpillars most of the diet of Yellow-billed Cuckoos. At night, Mexican Whip-poor-wills and Common Poorwills fly through the air with their mouths wide open, scooping up insects.

Because so much of their diet is insects, birds play a crucial role in controlling insect populations. That's one reason we construct bird boxes for Purple Martins and hope that Barn Swallows will build their mud nests under the eaves of our houses. It is estimated that an individual Purple Martin or Barn Swallow can eat up to a thousand insects a day. No wonder urban gardeners grow plants and flowers that attract insect-eating birds to control bugs, beetles, and worms. In Salt Lake City, there is a monument erected in honor of the California Gulls that swept in from the Great Salt Lake, helping to save the crops of Mormon pioneers from a devastating plague of crickets in 1848.

Forests benefit greatly from bird activity. Woodpeckers, in particular, are constantly grooming our forests, ridding them of bark beetles and other tree-killing insects. In Arizona, two woodpecker species, Hairy and American Three-toed, are well known for keeping outbreaks of forest insects in check. Locally, populations of these two species can increase dramatically during bark-beetle outbreaks. In urban areas, the sudden appearance of woodpeckers around the eaves and wood siding of a house alerts us to the presence of termites or other injurious insects.

Birds, especially raptors and owls, play an important role in controlling populations of rodents and small mammals. It's no accident that farmers and ranchers have always encouraged Barn Owls to nest in farm and ranch structures. Barn Owls are famous for their ability to hunt and find rodent prey in near-total darkness, utilizing special ear modifications. It is estimated that a single Barn Owl can consume up to 53 pounds of gopher in a single year.

Small mammal and rodent populations often fluctuate, and at times, there are population explosions. These outbreaks can present serious health hazards to humans, as these animals are known to carry diseases like bubonic plague and hantavirus. Raptors and owls play an important role in keeping them in check. Populations of some owl species, like Long-eared and Short-eared, can fluctuate dramatically in response to changes in rodent populations. Hawks also control populations of small mammals. In the spring, migrating Swanson's Hawks are often seen on berms in flooded agricultural fields west of Phoenix, feeding on gophers and mice whose burrows have been flooded by irrigation water.

Birding Arizona

Plant and flower pollination is another important activity of birds. Hummingbirds are probably the best known of the flower-pollinating birds. It's always fun watching them hovering and flying from bloom to bloom, their long bill and tongue probing the flowers of gilia and penstemon. Costa's Hummingbirds are particularly attracted to the flowers of the chuparosa plant, a bright red flower that takes its name from the Spanish word for hummingbird.

Through natural selection, many plants have evolved bright red- or orange-colored tubular flowers. Hummingbirds and other nectar feeders are the selecting agents that have helped shape, sculpt, and color many of these flowers. The relationship between hummingbirds and flowers is a codependent one whereby, in exchange for a supply of nectar, the hummingbird helps propagate the flowers. I once watched a female Lucifer Hummingbird coming to a feeder in the Chiricahua Mountains near Portal. At first I was confused, thinking it was some new species of yellow-billed hummingbird; that is, until I saw that her curved bill was completely covered with pollen.

One of the most interesting pollinators is the White-winged Dove. These large doves play an important role in the pollination and cross-pollination of the saguaro cactus. It is believed that their migration in springtime is timed to coincide with the reproductive cycle of these cacti, which bloom between April and June. You often see one of these doves perched atop a giant cactus, sipping the flower nectar, its bill and face covered with pollen. Later, the dove will eat the ripened red fruit and help disperse the seeds. One year, a White-winged Dove was so enthusiastic about a saguaro cactus in our yard that it built its nest right atop the plant. Unfortunately, the nest later had to be abandoned, as summer temperatures exceeded

Chapter 6

110 degrees.

Birds not only pollinate, but they also play an important role in replanting trees. As discussed in the section titled "Two Fascinating Arizona Corvids," two corvid species, Clark's Nutcracker and Pinyon Jay, are responsible for replanting many treeless areas in the West.

Vultures are not the prettiest of birds, but their interaction with the environment plays an important role in keeping our surroundings clean and free of disease. At one time or another, we have all been driving down a road and had to brake or swerve to avoid hitting Turkey or Black vultures that have gathered to eat the carcass of a road-killed rabbit, skunk, or snake.

The heads of the vulturine birds (Turkey and Black vultures and California Condors) are featherless, an adaptation that helps keep them free of harmful bacteria and viruses as they consume the decaying food or carrion that is the principal source of their diet. Turkey Vultures, in particular, have developed a highly refined sense of smell that enables them to find carrion. It is reported that gas companies have located pipeline leaks by watching for circling Turkey Vultures attracted by the putrid-smelling additive put in natural gas. Because they're able to locate carrion by smell, Turkey Vultures usually arrive to feed on carrion before Black Vultures, which do not use smell but watch and monitor the activity of the Turkey Vultures.

Besides the vultures, birds like herons, eagles, and hawks can also play an important part in cleaning up the environment. These birds are often seen eating dead and dying fish stranded in the receding waters of ponds, lakes, and canals. You can sometimes find rare species like Little Blue Heron or Reddish Egret by looking through flocks of herons feasting on dead and dying tilapia and carp caught in drying irrigation ditches and canals.

We've all heard of the proverbial canary miners used to carry with them into coal mines to detect the presence of dangerous gas. Today, we still use and rely on birds in a similar way. In the 1950s and 1960s, it was the Peregrine Falcon that first alerted us to the danger of widespread and excessive use of the pesticide DDT. As DDT entered the environment, one of its effects was to thin the eggshells of raptors, especially Peregrine Falcons, which suffered high mortality and a precipitous decline in numbers. Once DDT was banned, Peregrine Falcon populations rebounded. Today, these beautiful falcons are found in good numbers throughout Arizona.

Large die-offs of waterfowl and other birds often signal the presence of disease, poisons, and contaminants in our environment. We are sometimes alerted to the presence of West Nile virus by die-offs of birds, especially ravens, crows, and jays. Black-billed Magpies, which once occurred in small numbers in northeastern Arizona, seem to have recently suffered a severe population decline as a result of the West Nile virus. Large die-offs of Eared Grebes have alerted us to the presence of avian cholera and an infectious bacterial disease, erysipelas. Oil-coated and sick seabirds can alert us to undetected oil spills. A large die-off or movement of pelagic birds can sometimes signal problems with the ocean fish prey base. In 2008, for example, there was a large influx of Elegant Terns into southeastern Arizona. This seems to have coincided with the abandonment of the large tern nesting colony on Isla Raza in the Gulf of California, which in turn was due to a collapse of the fish prey base.

We sometimes use birds specifically as biological indicator species—those whose presence, absence, or relative well-being in the environment is an indicator or sign of the health of the ecosystem as a whole. An indicator species can signal a change in the biological condition of a particular ecosystem and thus can be used as a proxy to diagnose its health. In Arizona, the Forest Service uses the Northern Goshawk to indicate the presence (or absence) and health of old-growth forest.

The Northern Goshawk lives in an interesting and complex symbiotic relationship with old-growth ponderosa pine trees, tassel-eared squirrels, and forest mushrooms or truffles. The trees depend on the fungi to aid their roots in the uptake of water and nutrients, while the fungi depend on the squirrel to disperse their spores. The goshawk, in turn, often preys on the squirrel when it comes down to the ground in search of truffles. Both the goshawk and squirrel depend on the interlocking canopies of old-growth trees for nesting and cover. The Northern Goshawk population on Arizona's Kaibab Plateau—once considered the densest population anywhere—suffered a severe decline in the 1980s and 1990s as a result of the logging destruction of much of the area's old-growth ponderosa pine forest.

Birds play an increasingly important role as indicators of climate change. Climate change has the potential to seriously disrupt the behavior of birds in a variety of ways. A recent study by the National Audubon Society, based on Christmas Bird Count data, indicates that nearly 60 percent of the 305 species found wintering in North America have shifted their range northward by an average 35 miles. There is substantial evidence that some species, like Rose-breasted Grosbeak, Black-throated Blue Warbler, and Tree Swallow, are arriving on breeding grounds in the eastern United States at least three weeks earlier than normal. This may be an ominous sign. Many bird species time their migrations and arrival to breeding grounds to coincide with maximum food production. This is especially important for long-distance migrants like shorebirds, which migrate each spring to Arctic breeding grounds from as far away as the tip of South America. Global warming has the potential to seriously disrupt many of these ancient patterns of migratory behavior.

In Arizona, there is at least anecdotal evidence that climate change is increasingly disrupting and changing patterns of bird migration and distribution. Cliff Swallows appear to be arriving at least a month earlier in the springtime than they once did. Warmer winters probably account for the increased presence of overwintering species like Black-throated Gray Warbler, Wilson's Warbler, and Hammond's and Dusky flycatchers. Some species, like Greater Roadrunner and Crissal Thrasher, are extending their range and are now regularly found north of the Mogollon Rim. Climate change may account at least in part for increased sightings of Mexican species like Slate-throated Redstart, Sinaloa Wren, and Rufous-backed Robin. On the other hand, climate change resulting in warming winters and drought has the potential to seriously impact, if not extirpate, Arizona populations of Canada Jay, Pine Grosbeak, and Evening Grosbeak. A recent study links drought and extreme temperatures due to climate change to the continued decline of Arizona's Ferruginous Pygmy-Owl population. It's clear that birds are sending us a powerful message about climate change, and we would do well to listen.

Birds have also influenced us in many positive ways. They are often instrumental in bringing about changes in the attitudes and behavior of humans toward the environment. The preservation and conservation of bird species is a principal reason for the establishment of refuges and sanctuaries that not only benefit birds, but many other species. For example, the protection and conservation of birds figured prominently in the creation of the Buenos Aires National Wildlife Refuge, the San Pedro Riparian National Conservation Area, and a number of sanctuaries established by The Nature Conservancy, including the Hassayampa River Preserve and Patagonia-Sonoita Creek Preserve. On a local level, the protection and enjoyment of birds has figured prominently in the establishment, design, and operation of urban wildlife areas like Gilbert Water Ranch, the Tres Rios project in Phoenix, and Sweetwater Wetlands in Tucson.

As time goes by, we learn more and more about the important roles birds play in our natural world. In the next two sections, we'll look at the importance of preserving their habitat and try to draw some lessons from the fate of three extirpated species.

Habitat Matters

The famous ornithologist Roger Tory Peterson once wrote:
"the observation of birds leads
inevitably to environmental awareness."

When you think about it, it's easy to see why this is often the case. Birders look for birds in many different natural habitats, including grasslands, marshes, alpine tundra, desert scrub, and even on the ocean. They learn to identify the different trees in which they find birds and to recognize different plants and flowers that attract birds. With experience, birders come to appreciate how habitat complexity can affect the number and variety of bird species they encounter. Experienced birders recognize almost intuitively that the more varied and complex the habitat, the more niches it provides for the feeding and nesting requirements of different birds. On Breeding Bird Surveys in the pine forests of northern Arizona, I always found more bird species in complex forest habitat, where there was a mixture of tree species of different sizes and age classes, than in uniformly even-aged forest.

Watching birds heightens our awareness and appreciation for many complex biological relationships that exist in the natural world. Birders learn, for example, that fires are often vital for forest health, providing, among other things, dead trees for cavity-nesting species like Western Bluebird, American Kestrel, and Purple Martin, and the occasional insect bonanzas for woodpeckers. That's why American Three-toed and Hairy woodpeckers are often much easier to find in fire-burned areas for the first two or three years following forest fires. Birders learn that scarcity of food in the far north can result in irruptions that bring rare birds like Bohemian Waxwings into our state in the winter, and that an increase in rodent populations can result in increased numbers of Long-eared and Short-eared Owls. Recently, birders have become aware of how the intentional introduction of a leaf-eating beetle to control tamarisk may seriously jeopardize critical nesting habitat for the endangered Southwestern Willow Flycatcher, and how lead introduced into the environment threatens ongoing attempts to successfully reintroduce the endangered California Condor.

Birding also makes us aware of how easily the environment can be altered, degraded, or destroyed. For example, how often have

Audubon chapters had to redraw Christmas count circles because of increased urbanization or conversion of habitat to farmland or housing tracts? How many times have you gone out to a favorite riparian area to look for spring migrants, only to find the area stripped bare by cattle that have broken through fences, or traveled to a favorite wetland to look for shorebirds, only to find it pumped dry or the water diverted?

I will never forget watching my first Ferruginous Pygmy-Owl in a saguaro cactus in the Tucson foothills in 1987. At the time, the area was beautiful upper Sonoran Desert habitat, with only a scattering of dwellings in the distance. On a return visit several years ago, I found the saguaro gone and the area engulfed by endless rows of houses. Yes, birding does lead to environmental awareness, but sometimes that awareness can be very painful.

Perhaps nothing underscores this point more forcefully than the loss of riparian habitat that has occurred over the past century in Arizona. Riparian habitats are the vegetative areas that grow along the edges of rivers and streams and around lakes and ponds. No other North American habitat is home to a greater diversity of plant, animal, and bird life. To appreciate how dramatically it has diminished in Arizona, one only has to look at the map of significant riparian areas in the *Arizona Breeding Bird Atlas*. Along rivers like the Santa Cruz, Gila, Salt, and Verde, there remain only scattered pockets of riparian habitat. The lower Colorado River and its delta were once home to riparian forests that harbored jaguars and immense flocks of migrating waterfowl. Aldo Leopold, the famous writer, naturalist, and conservationist, on a canoe trip to the area in 1922 described it as "honey wilderness." In their book, the authors of the *Birds of the Lower Colorado River* describe the area today:

Birding Arizona

"To summarize the vegetative changes that have occurred, a floodplain that was once filled end to end with expansive and impenetrable forests of cottonwood, willow, and mesquite has been converted in little more than a century to a largely treeless valley dominated by farms and towns. The relatively little remaining riparian vegetation exists in fragmented strips and islands, most being salt cedar."

The story is similar along the Gila River. By 1900, the Gila's surface flow had been drastically reduced. As groundwater levels dropped, riparian communities disappeared. Describing what the river was once like, C. H. Lowe wrote in *The Vertebrates of Arizona*:

"Along the formerly great Gila River (the now dry bed of which stretches across the Sonoran Desert of western Arizona) there were extensive marshes, swamps, and floodplains with cattail (*Typha domingensis*), bulrush (*Scirpus olneyi*), giant reed (*Arunda donax*), commonreed (*Phragmites communis*), arrowweed (*Pluchea sericea),* and many trees. The dense vegetation of these well-developed riparian communities often stood 10–15 feet [3–4.5 m] high and supported a tremendous quantity and variety of wildlife."

It is estimated that over 90 percent of Arizona's native riparian habitat has been lost or seriously degraded over the past hundred years, mostly as a result of dam building, groundwater pumping, overgrazing, and diversions of water for industrial and municipal uses.

Birders have a significant stake in the preservation of remaining riparian habitats. After all, these greenbelts provide critical nesting habitat for many of our favorite species. The Patagonia-Sonoita Creek Preserve in southeastern Arizona is a good example. This area was on the verge of development when it was purchased by The Nature Conservancy and Tucson Audubon Society in 1968. Its acquisition saved for future generations outstanding cottonwood- willow habitat along perennially flowing Sonoita Creek. Birders now come here from around the country, even from around the world, to look for the many specialty species that nest along the creek. They include Thick-billed and Tropical kingbirds, Rose-throated Becard, Gray Hawk, and Yellow-billed Cuckoo. This area has produced several very rare species, including Yellow Grosbeak, Black-capped Gnatcatcher, Fan-tailed Warbler, Blue Mockingbird, and the first US records of Sinaloa Wren and Cinnamon Hummingbird.

The Santa Cruz is another river that has lost most of its riparian habitat. It flows north out of Mexico to eventually join the Gila River. Along most of its course, it is now a dry, empty riverbed, devoid of vegetation. However, a 15-mile stretch between Nogales and Tubac has permanent running water, thanks to releases from the Nogales wastewater treatment plant. The area along this stretch of river boasts a lush cottonwood-willow gallery forest. This area dramatically demonstrates the importance of these river systems and their riparian plant communities, not only for nesting bird species, but for many migrating species that use it during spring and fall.

In early March, this 15-mile stretch of the Santa Cruz River attracts migrating Common Black-Hawks as they migrate from Mexico to spread out and nest along creeks and rivers across central Arizona. In addition to the hawks, migrating neotropical birds are attracted to the area's lush vegetation. In spring and fall, waves of migrating flycatchers, tanagers, vireos, warblers, and sparrows stop to rest and feed, gleaning insects from the leaves of the cottonwood and willow trees. One spring morning, a friend and I witnessed a mini-fallout of migrating "empids," a group of notoriously diffi-cult-to-identify flycatchers of the genus *Empidonax*. They seemed to be flitting about and perching on just about every tree and bush. We identified five different species. During spring and fall migra-tion, this area is one of the best places in Arizona to look for eastern warblers and rare vagrants.

The San Pedro River is often described as the Southwest's last free-flowing desert river. It has some of the finest remaining riparian habitat left in Arizona. In 1988, the San Pedro Riparian National Conservation Area was established to protect a 36-mile segment of the river from the US–Mexico border to near St. David. Not long after establishment of the national conservation area, the river's badly overgrazed and damaged riparian habitat made a comeback. Soon, cottonwood and willows were regenerating, and grasses and emergent vegetation began to flourish.

During the 1980s and 1990s, one of my favorite Mexican species, the Green Kingfisher, began to make regular appearances on the restored San Pedro, even nesting in the area. The lush ripar-ian gallery forest along the San Pedro is one of the last strongholds of the distinct western population of Yellow-billed Cuckoo. This cuckoo is also known as the "rain crow," for its tendency to sing be-fore rain storms. This bird received official designation as a threat-ened species under the Endangered Species Act in 2014.

Today, however, the San Pedro and its riparian habitat are once again in jeopardy; this time, from groundwater pumping to satisfy the needs of nearby Sierra Vista and Fort Huachuca. Pump-ing has caused a diminished subterranean flow feeding into the river. As a result, the river has been on the verge of going dry at times during the second decade of the 2000s.

Many of our favorite Arizona birding spots, particularly riparian areas, are in constant jeopardy and in need of protection. The fight to save and preserve them is one that must be waged constantly. For example, after years of effort, including numerous lawsuits, environmentalists succeeded in protecting important riparian areas along the Verde River from construction of habitat-destroying dams. The Verde River is the stronghold of southwestern desert-nesting Bald Eagles, which as of 2018 numbered about 90 pairs. These eagles have evolved a number of adaptations that help them survive in a desert environment: they are smaller, nest earlier in the spring, and unlike other Bald Eagles, sometimes build their nests on cliff faces. This unique population depends on healthy riparian habitat for nesting and foraging.

Today, however, the river faces multiple threats: everything from groundwater pumping, which threatens to dry it up in the summertime, to feral horses that run loose and eat young cottonwood and willow trees. To get an appreciation for the value of this cottonwood-willow habitat along the Verde to migrating and nesting birds, visit Box Bar Recreation Area or Needle Rock Recreation Area some spring or fall morning. The trees in these areas can be alive with passerines moving in migration along the river.

Riparian areas are not our only endangered habitats. Excessive commercial logging of national forests during the 1980s and 1990s resulted in the loss of much of the Southwest's old-growth forest. In addition, shortsighted fire-suppression policies, an ongoing drought, and the effects of global climate change have increased the severity of forest fires. These impacts affected and will continue to affect many bird species, including two of my favorites, the Mexican Spotted Owl and the Northern Goshawk.

The Mexican Spotted Owl is a subspecies of the Spotted Owl. Many birders see their life Spotted Owl in southeastern Arizona, where it can be found in narrow, shady canyons in isolated mountain ranges like the Chiricahuas and Huachucas. In northern Arizona, however, its preferred habitat is dense, uneven-aged forest with multilayered closed canopy. These forest characteristics are found in old-growth mixed-conifer forest in excess of 200 years old. Intensive logging of this habitat led to the owl's being listed as a threatened species in 1993.

The north Kaibab National Forest was once home to one of the densest populations of Northern Goshawks found anywhere. These beautiful accipiters hunt and nest in old-growth ponderosa pine forest with high canopy closure. A relatively long tail and short wings help them fly through the trees in pursuit of prey. Heavy logging has resulted in a precipitous decline in nesting pairs.

Grasslands are one of my favorite places to watch birds, but like riparian and old-growth forest habitats, they are also endangered and in need of protection. In Arizona, grasslands can be found in many parts of the state. They occur over a wide range— from alpine meadows to low-elevation semidesert grasslands. Wherever you find them, chances are you will find good birds.

I especially like to bird grasslands in the winter, when there is an influx of visiting species—everything from sparrows to hawks and owls. In grassland areas between Flagstaff and Winslow, I like to look for Chestnut-collared Longspurs and an occasional Lapland Longspur. The beautiful grasslands of the San Rafael Valley in southeastern Arizona are famous for harboring such wintering species as Baird's Sparrow, Sprague's Pipit, Chestnut-collared Longspur, Short-eared Owl, and Rough-legged Hawk. In summertime, grasslands in northern Arizona fill with the beautiful songs of Vesper and Lark sparrows. In the grasslands of southeastern Arizona, you can hear Botteri's and Cassin's sparrows, which begin singing with the first drops of rain from the summer monsoon. Many of our favorite species nest and can be found year-round in grasslands, including Grasshopper Sparrow, Horned Lark, and Western and Eastern meadowlarks.

Grasslands habitats have been severely impacted by the introduction of non-native grass species, disruption of fire regimes, conversion of grasslands to shrub and pinyon-juniper habitat, and especially, overgrazing by livestock. Livestock grazing resulted in the extirpation of the beautiful, almost mythical, Masked Bobwhite from the savanna-like grasslands of south-central Arizona by the turn of the century, and is thought to be a major contributor to the disappearance of the Aplomado Falcon, which once nested in the grasslands of Cochise County. The great Arizona naturalist Herbert Brown summed it up well in commenting on the disappearance of the Masked Bobwhite: "From time immemorial it had thrived in the prosperous grassland of the border but it died off almost instantly with the demise of its home with the coming of the great herds and their owners. Let those who really want to conserve our wild heritage ponder well the lesson."

The *Arizona Breeding Bird Atlas* notes that overgrazing has had a major adverse impact on virtually all types of grassland habitat. In 1996, an Arizona Game and Fish Department study cited overgrazing as an impact contributing to the endangerment of 23 out of 29 of Arizona's threatened and endangered listed birds, including many of our favorite nesting and wintering grassland species.

Finally, let's not forget our urban habitats. Urban environments are home to a surprisingly large and diverse community of birds. In his book *Welcome to Subirdia*, John Marzluff writes in fascinating detail about the many bird species that have adapted to and exploited the varied habitats we have created in our cities. They include not only common and familiar species like House Sparrow, Starling, and Rock Pigeon, which thrive in human presence, but a whole suite of native species that have been able to adapt to urban living.

In urban areas of Arizona, water and irrigation have facilitated the planting of myriad exotic and native plant species, creating a mosaic of habitats that provide the insects, fruit, and seeds for a number of native birds. They include such species as Abert's Towhee, Curve-billed Thrasher, Verdin, White-winged Dove, Northern Cardinal, Cactus Wren, and Gila Woodpecker. Metropolitan Phoenix is home to an impressive number of native species. In fact, I can go out my front door in Phoenix on any given day and see or hear at least 15 different bird species.

We can do a number of things to ensure the continued well-being of these urban-adapted species. They include planting vegetation that will create a diversity of habitats within landscapes, keeping cats indoors, providing food, and working with urban planners to provide connectivity with surrounding desert areas and water sources.

If we are to protect threatened and endangered habitats and

preserve them for future generations, birders must become environmentally active. It's not enough to be environmentally aware. The assault on our environment is ongoing and continuous. I encourage all birders to contribute to and actively support environmental organizations such as national and local Audubon Societies, the Sierra Club, The Nature Conservancy, and the Center for Biological Diversity, which are working to preserve threatened and endangered habitats.

Reintroduced Species: A Cautionary Tale

In August 1982, a group of birders from the Maricopa Audubon Society traveled to Mount Pinos in Los Padres National Forest north of Los Angeles to look for the California Condor. At the time, there were only 22 California Condors left in the wild, and an intense debate raged over whether they should remain in the wild or be trapped and taken in for captive breeding.

Late in the morning of August 18, our group spotted two condors far off in the distance, floating on the rising thermals. Through spotting scopes, we could see flashes of white in the wing linings and secondaries as they banked and turned. Standing there, I never dreamed that the next time I would see one of these magnificent birds would be almost 25 years later in northern Arizona. On a hot August afternoon in 2008, I was parked at Navajo Bridge over Marble Canyon, eating a sandwich, when I spotted two California Condors circling high overhead, drifting toward the Vermilion Cliffs.

The California Condor, Masked Bobwhite, and Thick-billed Parrot are three birds that wildlife officials have attempted to reintroduce into Arizona in areas where they once occurred. This section is subtitled "A Cautionary Tale" because these attempted reintroductions have had very limited success. With two of them— the Masked Bobwhite and Thick-billed Parrot—reintroduction efforts have so far been unsuccessful. While the reintroduction of the California Condor shows promise, it is still very much an open question whether it will ultimately succeed. Behind the partial success and failures, there are important lessons to be learned.

Arizona was home to the California Condor throughout most of the Pleistocene. We know this from condor bones excavated in dry caves in the Grand Canyon, most of which date from over 10,000 years ago. The large extinction of megafauna at the end of the Pleistocene is thought to have shrunk the condor's range to an area from northern Baja California to southern British Columbia. That range gradually contracted, mostly as a result of shooting and poisoning, to where, by the 1930s, the California Condor was found only in Central California.

In modern times, condors still visited Arizona on occasion, with a few sight records in the 1880s and another sight record from as recently as 1924. It was not surprising, then, that the Grand Canyon region was selected in 1996 as a release site for reintroduction using captive-bred birds.

California Condors are one of our largest birds—much larger than Bald or Golden eagles. Adults have a wingspan of almost nine feet and can weigh as much as 23 pounds. They are carrion eaters that depend on dead carcasses for most of their food. Condors are a long-lived species with low reproductive rates: they do not sexually mature until age six or seven, and they only mate every other year. They can live up to 60 years in the wild.

In 1996, an experimental group of six captive-bred California Condors was released near the Vermilion Cliffs National Monument in northern Arizona. In November 2003, a pair of released birds successfully fledged a chick in a cave in the Grand Canyon. It was celebrated as the first non-captive-bred condor to appear in Arizona in over a hundred years. As of 2018, there are about 80 California Condors in the Arizona-Utah population. While this may sound very encouraging, the ultimate fate of this species—at least in Arizona and Utah—remains very much in doubt. This is due primarily to lead poisoning.

California Condors are highly sensitive to lead, with that heavy metal being the number one cause of premature death of reintroduced birds. Since 1996, 189 captive-bred condors have been released in Arizona. Of the 119 deaths where a cause of death has been established, 60 deaths, or 53 percent, were a result of lead poisoning. At any given time, about 30 percent of the released population has to be treated for lead poisoning. The reintroduced condor that managed to survive the longest in Arizona was a female bird that successfully reproduced. She died at age 16, far short of the 60-year life span of wild condors. That bird had to be treated for lead poisoning more than a dozen times.

The principal source of lead in their environment is from lead bullets. The condors eat and ingest lead and lead fragments from bullets while scavenging and eating entrails left by hunters after they clean their deer and other game. There is a high correlation between condor poisoning and the hunting season. To try to remedy the problem, the Arizona Game and Fish Department has instituted a voluntary non-lead ammunition program for hunts in the core of the condors' range. The department supplies hunters with free, non-lead ammunition. While participation in this voluntary program has been encouraging, it remains to be seen whether it will ultimately reduce condor fatalities and whether we will once again have a viable, free-flying population.

The Masked Bobwhite is an endangered subspecies of the Northern Bobwhite. The males have cinnamon-red underparts and black heads and throats that give them a masked look. The females' plumage is almost identical to that of the female Northern Bobwhite. Like the Northern Bobwhite, the Masked Bobwhite gives a call that sounds like its name, a whistled "bob whoit." The call is often given by males from a conspicuous perch at the onset of the nesting season. Most of the time, these birds tend to be secretive and elusive, making them hard to find in their preferred grassland habitat.

Up until the 1880s, Masked Bobwhite were reportedly common in parts of southern Arizona, where they were restricted to shrubby grasslands in the Altar and Santa Cruz valleys. However, with the coming of large-scale cattle grazing in the 1890s, the Masked Bobwhite population quickly plummeted, and not long after that, the birds were extirpated from Arizona. Experimental releases followed at various times in ensuing decades without success. Today, only a very small number of Masked Bobwhite, if any, are left in the wild. Small populations may be hanging on in a few isolated areas of Sonora, Mexico.

In 1984, the US Fish and Wildlife Service purchased the

Chapter 6

Buenos Aires Ranch in southeastern Arizona, in hopes that the Masked Bobwhite could be successfully reintroduced onto the ranch's grasslands. Like most birders, I never saw a Masked Bobwhite in the wild in its native habitat. The closest I ever got was looking at caged, captive-bred birds awaiting release at the Buenos Aires while I was on a visit to the area in search of a rare Garganey duck that had dropped into a pond on the ranch property in 1986.

Between 1986 and 2006, 22,000 captive-bred Masked Bobwhite were released on the Buenos Aires National Wildlife Refuge. Unfortunately, none these birds survived. Causes of this failure are not fully understood, although it appears there are a number of factors at work. One of the reasons seems to be climate change, which has increased the frequency of dry winters. In springtime, the quail depend on emerging vegetation and insects from winter rain to tide them over until the beginning of the summer rain, which is also the beginning of the birds' nesting season. Frequent dry winters have resulted in less food and high quail mortality.

It is also believed that the ranch's habitat never fully recovered from heavy grazing. One of the consequences of grazing has been the incursion of mesquite trees, which may provide a hunting advantage for perching avian predators like hawks. Another factor is that captive-bred birds often have problems adjusting to the wild when released. Captive breeding breeds the "wildness" out of the birds, making it hard for them to survive on their own.

The refuge is now in the middle of a habitat restoration project intended to ameliorate some of these problems. Until that slow and expensive process is finished, however, efforts will be made to concentrate on Masked Bobwhite recovery in more suitable habitat in Mexico. The Buenos Aires refuge will continue to be the focal point for reintroduction in the United States.

Unlike the California Condor and Masked Bobwhite, there is little documented evidence that the Thick-billed Parrot ever nested in Arizona, although these parrots are well documented as visitors to the Chiricahua Mountains—sometimes in the hundreds—until well into the 1930s. They probably visited during periods of food stress in their nesting areas.

Thick-billed Parrots nest in the northern Sierra Madre of Mexico. In fact, they nest so close to Arizona that some of their mountain breeding areas in Mexico can be seen from the tops of the Chiricahua Mountains. More than likely, they were hunted to extinction in Arizona, and roaming flocks never reestablished contact with the Chiricahua or other southeastern Arizona mountains.

What a treat it would have been to see large flocks of these bright-green parrots in the pine forests of southeastern Arizona! Thick-billed Parrots are macaw-sized birds that have a dark-red forehead and fore-crown and a red bend in the wings. They are exceptionally strong fliers, often flying like geese in tight V formations. They live in large flocks and often nest in aspen snags, using abandoned woodpecker holes. They wander widely in search of their preferred foods, which are various types of pine seeds.

Thick-billed Parrots are intelligent and highly social. Individual parrots will often alert other members of the flock when danger is near. Much of this behavior has to be learned. For example, eating pine seeds is a complicated procedure, whereby the parrot must snip the pine cone off a branch with its large beak. It then grasps the cone with its feet while using its beak to shred the cone from bottom to top, extracting the seeds with its tongue. This complicated activity must be taught to young parrots by adults. When it comes to reintroduction, this behavioral sophistication can be a disadvantage, especially with captive-bred birds.

Between 1986 and 1993, attempts were made to reintroduce Thick-billed Parrots into the Chiricahua Mountains. In all, 88 birds were released, including a number of captive-bred birds. These releases proved to be unsuccessful because there were too few wild birds and the captive-bred birds had insufficient survival skills. They were unable to learn wild behavior and to protect themselves from predators. Many fell victim to Northern Goshawks and Red-tailed Hawks.

Some of the Thick-billed Parrots flew out of the Chiricahuas and ended up spending the summer on the Mogollon Rim. Several of my friends reported seeing them in the pines along the road to Young, south of Payson. These birds eventually succumbed to a combination of drought, which reduced the availability of pine cones, and a huge fire that burned much of the area's pine forest.

As these three species illustrate, reintroduction can be a complicated, costly, and problematic undertaking. Before we can successfully reintroduce bird species that have been lost, we must first try to understand why they vanished from particular areas in the first place. The answers are probably more complex than many people think.

Habitat loss is certainly a major and overarching reason why we have lost species. However, there are other factors at work. Some of them include human predation (shooting, trapping, and collecting), disease, environmental contaminants, and introduced ators. In the case of the Thick-billed Parrot, it was probably human predation (shooting) that caused or contributed to their extirpation from the mountains of southeastern Arizona. With the California Condor, it was poisons in their diet and shooting, and not primarily habitat loss, that brought them to nearly complete extinction in much of their range. With the Masked Bobwhite, on the other hand, it was clearly habitat loss and degradation, given the strong correlation between the arrival of large-scale cattle grazing and plummeting quail population at the beginning of the 1900s.

We should never be lulled into thinking that if a species is lost from an area, we can always reintroduce it in the same or similar habitat somewhere else. It's not simply a matter of finding what appears to be suitable habitat and releasing birds. There are many inhibiting factors that can prevent successful species reintroduction. The Masked Bobwhite is a case in point. Climate change and drought, changes to grassland habitat from past heavy grazing, and the inability of captive-bred birds to adjust to the wild are some of the factors that may be inhibiting their successful reintroduction. With the Thick-billed Parrot, there were a number of complicating factors, including the inability of released captive-bred birds to properly flock, forage, and protect themselves from predators. With the California Condor, the problem is not lack of suitable habitat, but the presence of lead in the environment.

Arizona ranks third in the nation in the number of native bird species. Today, however, many of these species face an uncertain future as ongoing drought and climate change accelerate the loss of critical nesting and wintering habitats. The Condor, Parrot, and Bobwhite remind us that we must act decisively if we are to ensure that more species do not disappear from our state in the future.

accidental
a descriptive term for a bird that is seen far from its normal range and not to be expected there again

accipiter
a genus of short-winged hawks that includes Goshawk, Cooper's, and Sharp-shinned, well adapted to darting through forests.

alcid
a bird of the family Alcidae (web-footed birds with short legs and wings)

Arizona specialty: a highly sought-after bird found in Arizona

barranca: Spanish word for a ravine or gorge

basic plumage: the feather pattern seen in birds outside of breeding season

big day: usually a team effort, it's a 24-hour period during which the primary objective is to identify as many bird species as possible

big year: an effort to find as many bird species as possible in a given area in a calendar year

Birdathon: a fundraising event where pledges of money are made to birders based on the number of species they find and identify

boreal: habitat and climate commonly associated with northern Canada

breeding plumage: the feather pattern seen in birds during breeding season, also known as "alternate plumage"

buteo: a genus of broad-winged hawks, well adapted to soaring

call note: in contrast to birdsong, a brief sound with a relatively simple acoustic structure

cere: the area of bare skin around the beak

citizen scientist: nonprofessional who gathers and collects data for professionals to analyze and use

color morph: refers to any one of the color phases that exist in a bird population (as in the light and dark morphs seen in many hawks)

Corvids: A family of birds (Corvidae) that includes among others crows and jays; Clark's Nutcracker and Pinyon Jay are corvids

covert: small feathers that cover the bases of large ones on the wings and tail

emergent: plants rooted in the water whose leaves and stems grow out of the water

empid: a small flycatcher of the genus *Empidonax*

endemic: a species restricted to a given area

extirpated: a species that no longer occurs in a given area.

fallout: when migrating birds are forced to come to rest in an area due to a severe weather disturbance

first fall: a bird born in the spring or summer, now living through its first autumn

first state record: a state's first documented and accepted record of a bird species

flight call: sound made by a bird in flight

genus: a group of related species descended from a common ancestor

granary, granaries: trees or utility poles with holes drilled by Acorn Woodpeckers, into which they pound acorns to store them for the winter

hot spot: an area where birders have found a number of rare and unusual birds

hypothetical species: a species that has been reported with substantial documentation but not supported by a specimen, photograph, or multiple observations

irrupt: make an irregular migration

irruption: an often spectacular southward mass movement of birds in fall and winter

Jurassic Period: a geologic period that occurred between 201.3 million years ago and 145 million years ago, in which dinosaurs came to be the dominant fauna

kettle: a group of birds wheeling and circling in the air like boiling water

life bird: a new bird that can be added to one's life list

life list: the list of bird species seen during years or a lifetime

of birding

locally: in a very small or localized area

mandible: the upper and lower half of a bird's bill

Mesozoic Era: an interval of geologic time from about 252 to 66 million years ago. Also called the age of reptiles

migrant: a bird that for various reasons moves from one area to another

migrant trap: oasis of trees and water that attracts migrating and vagrant birds

morph: see "color morph"

neotropical migrant: a bird that migrates northward after wintering in Mexico, Central America, or South America

non-breeding: a bird's plumage retained throughout the non-breeding season

old growth: forests distinguished by old trees and encompassing the later stages of a tree community with accumulated dead, woody material

park: a large mountain meadow

passage migrant: a bird that does not nest locally but only passes through on the way to its breeding grounds

passerine: a perching bird

pelagic: an ocean-going bird

pishing: making a noise that sounds something like the hissing sound made at a villain in a movie, to attract birds

post-breeding dispersal: the action taken by birds when they wander away from breeding grounds and habitats after they finish nesting

raptor: a diurnal bird of prey such as a hawk, eagle, falcon, or vulture

rare: present in an area but infrequently seen

rarity: a bird that is a surprise to see but not out of its normal range

resident: a non-migratory bird that stays in one area year-round

riparian: relating to habitat adjacent to rivers and streams

scapular: a group of feathers that originate at the shoulder, which vary in prominence from group to group

shorebirds: a large group of small to medium-sized birds with relatively thin bills and long legs that feed on aquatic insects and other invertebrates on shores and mudflats

song: the musical vocalizations of a bird, usually a male, made to attract a mate and defend territory

songbird: a passerine that sings

a song to defend a territory or attract a mate

split: a bird species that has been divided into two separate species

state bird: a bird seen for the first time in a given state (e.g., "my first state Northern Cardinal")

sublingual pouch: a special elastic structure at the back of the mouth that allows Pinyon Jays and Clark's Nutcrackers to hold and transport large numbers of seeds

Triassic Period: a geologic period that occurred between 251 and 199 million years ago, marked by the first emergence of dinosaurs

vagrant: a bird that has wandered outside its normal range or area of occurrence

waterfowl: a term generally applied to ducks, geese, and swans

wintering: spending the winter months in a particular area

Arizona Game and Fish Department. 1996. "Wildlife of Special Concern in Arizona." Phoenix: Arizona Game and Fish Department.

Balda, Russell P., and Alan Kamil. 2006. "Linking Life Zones, Life History Traits, Ecology, and Spatial Cognition in Four Allopatric Southwestern Seed Caching Corvids." 2006. Papers in Behavior and Biological Sciences. Lincoln: Univ. of Nebraska. http://digitalcommons.unl.edu/bioscibehavior/3

Beckman, Craig W., and Anna K. Lindholm. 1991. "The Advantages and Evolution of a Morphological Novelty." Nature 349: 519–20.

Brown, David E. 1989. *Arizona Game Birds*. Tucson: Univ. of Arizona Press.

Brown, Matthew C., and Robin A. Baker. 2009. "First United States Record of Sinaloa Wren (*Thryothorus sinaloa*)." North American Birds 63: 196–201

Chronic, Halka. 1983. *Roadside Geology of Arizona*. Missoula: Mountain Press.

Corman Troy E., and Catherine Wise-Gervais. 2005. *Arizona Breeding Bird Atlas*. Albuquerque: Univ. of New Mexico Press.

Epple, Anne O. 1995. *A Field Guide to the Plants of Arizona*. Guilford, CT: Globe Pequot Press.

Fischer, Dan L. 2001. *Early Southwest Ornithologists 1528–1900*. Tucson: Univ. of Arizona Press.

Flesch, Aaron D. 2014. "Spatiotemporal Trends and Drivers of Population Dynamics in a Declining Sonoran Predator." Biological Conservation 175: 110–18.

Glinsky, Richard L., ed. 1998. *The Raptors of Arizona*. Tucson: Univ. of Arizona Press.

Jacobs, Brad. *Birding on the Navajo and Hopi Reservations*. 1986. Sycamore, MO: Jacobs Pub. Co.

Krueper, David, Jonathan Bart, and Terrell D. Rich. 2003. "Response of Vegetation and Breeding Birds to the Removal of Cattle on the San Pedro River, Arizona." Conserv. Biol. 17 (2): 607–15.

Lowe, Charles H., ed. 1964. *The Vertebrates of Arizona*. Tucson: Univ of Arizona Press.

Marzluff, John M. 2014. *Welcome to Subirdia*. New Haven: Yale University Press.

Monson, Gale, and Allan R. Phillips. 1981. *Annotated Checklist of the Birds of Arizona*. Tucson: Univ. of Arizona Press.

Phillips, Allan R., Joe Marshall, and Gale Monson. 1964. *The Birds of Arizona*. Tucson: Univ of Arizona Press.

Rea, Amadeo M. 1983. *Once a River*. Tucson: Univ. of Arizona Press.

Rosenberg, Kenneth V., Robert D. Ohmart, William C. Hunter, and Bertin W. Anderson. 1991. *Birds of the Lower Colorado River Valley*. Tucson: Univ. of Arizona Press.

Sibley, David A. 2014. *The Sibley Guide to Birds, Second Edition*. New York: Alfred A. Knopf.

Snyder, Noel F. R., Susan Koenig, James Koschmann, Helen A. Snyder, and Terry B. Johnson. 1994. "Thick-billed Parrot Releases in Arizona." Condor 96: 845–62.

Snyder, Noel F.R., and Helen Snyder. 2000. *The California Condor: A Saga of Natural History and Conservation*. San Diego: Academic Press.

Weiner, Jonathan. 1995. *The Beak of the Finch*. New York: Vintage Books.

Witzeman, Janet, Salome Demaree, and Eleanor Radke. 1997. *Birds of Phoenix and Maricopa County, Arizona*. Phoenix: Maricopa Audubon Society.

Zimmer, Kevin J. 1985. *The Western Bird Watcher: An Introduction to Birding in the American West*. Englewood Cliffs, NJ: Prentice Hall.

ACKNOWLEDGMENTS

I wish to thank the following friends and fellow birders who supplied information, advice, or reviewed portions of the manuscript: Russ Balda, Troy Corman, Henry Detwiler, Rich Hoyer, Chuck LaRue, Michael Moore, Duane Morse, Laurie Nessel, David Pearson, David Stejskal, Mark Stevenson, David Vander Pluym. I owe a special debt of gratitude to Julie Hammonds for her invaluable suggestions, advice and help in the preparation of the manuscript.

I also want to acknowledge R. W. Morse Company for agreeing to publish my manuscript and bringing along other members of their team such as Laura Lavington for manuscript review, Paul Biniasz for map designs and Christina Merwin for her overall design.

Finally - thanks to my wife Eleanor, for her unwavering support on this project and her painting of the Grace's Warbler for the cover.

Mogollon Rim

About the Author

Charles J. Babbitt is a third generation Arizonan. He is a lawyer, past president of the Maricopa Audubon Society and past member of the Arizona Bird Committee. He is a recipient of the 1999 George B. Fell Award (Natural Areas Association) "in recognition of a lifetime of professional work and personal effort dedicated to the protection and stewardship of the natural areas of Arizona and the Colorado Plateau." He has served on the boards of directors of various non-profit environmental organizations including the Land and Water Trust Fund of the Rockies, Arizona - New Mexico Parks and Conservation Association, Southwest Forest Alliance and the Sonoran Desert National Park Advisory Board. A well-respected writer and field trip leader, he's birded in Arizona for over 40 years.